Chikahito Harada

Russia and North-east Asia

T0386175

LONDON AND NEW YORK

Adelphi Paper 310

First published July 1997 by **Oxford University Press** for
The International Institute for Strategic Studies
23 Tavistock Street, London WC2E 7NQ

This reprint published by Routledge
2 Park Square, Milton Park, Abingdon, Oxon, OX14 4RN
For the International Institute for Strategic Studies
Arundel House, 13-15 Arundel Street, Temple Place, London, WC2R 3DX
www.iiss.org

Simultaneously published in the USA and Canada
By Routledge
711 Third Avenue, New York, NY 10017

Routledge is an imprint of the Taylor & Francis Group, an informa business

© The International Institute for Strategic Studies 1997

Director Dr John Chipman
Deputy Director Rose Gottemoeller
Editor Dr Gerald Segal
Assistant Editor Rachel Neaman
Design and Production Mark Taylor

All rights reserved. No part of this publication may be reproduced, stored in a retrieval system or transmitted in any form or by any means, electronic, mechanical or photo-copying, recording or otherwise, without the prior permission of the International Institute for Strategic Studies. Within the UK, exceptions are allowed in respect of any fair dealing for the purpose of research or private study, or criticism or review, as permitted under the Copyright, Designs and Patents Act, 1988, or in the case of reprographic reproduction in accordance with the terms of the licences issued by the Copyright Licensing Agency. Enquiries concerning reproduction outside these terms and in other countries should be sent to the publisher.

This book is sold subject to the condition that it shall not, by way of trade or otherwise, be lent, re-sold, hired out or otherwise circulated without the publisher's prior consent in any form of binding or cover other than that in which it is published and without a similar condition including this condition being imposed on the subsequent purchaser.

British Library Cataloguing in Publication Data
Data available

Library of Congress Cataloguing in Publication Data
ISBN: 978-0-19-829402-3

contents

maps & tables

Acknowledgements

The author would like to express his deep appreciation to the Directing Staff of the International Institute for Strategic Studies for their valuable advice and comments on earlier drafts of this paper, and to his Foreign Ministry colleagues – especially Ichiro Kawabata and Yoshihiro Yamamura – for their warm support. His thanks also go to his wife, Atsuko, for her constant encouragement.

Map I *The Russian Federation*

East Siberian Sea

Bering
Sea

FEDERATION

Sea of
Okhotsk

Krasnoyarsk

Lake
Baikal

Vladivostok

Sea of
Japan

JAPAN

Tokyo

Ulan Bator

NORTH
KOREA

MONGOLIA

Pyongyang Seoul

Beijing

SOUTH
KOREA

CHINA

Yellow
Sea

East
China
Sea

Since the collapse of the Soviet Union in 1991, the Russian leadership
has had to reconcile major internal differences over the nature of its
domestic policies, while developing a foreign policy that realistically
serves its national interests. The first few years of independence
were characterised by wide-ranging internal debate about the
direction of Russia's political and economic reforms, and about what
constituted its international interests. Today, nearly six years after
the end of the Union, the post-Soviet transformation of Russia's
foreign policy is still not complete. In the country's foreign-policy
communities, its status as a 'great power' and its 'equitable partnership' with the other major international powers have become clichés,
but its political élite, still seeking a clear identity, remains undecided
on what direction to follow. Russia's domestic politics and the rise of
conservatism and nationalism have greatly influenced its foreign-
policy shift away from its initial Western orientation. The political
imperatives to diversify its foreign policy have led Russia to activate
its diplomacy towards the countries of North-east Asia – China,
Japan and the two Koreas.

Although Russia has retained its traditional interest in
establishing a strong foothold or sphere of influence in North-east
Asia, it has not succeeded in doing so in any meaningful way. In
1991, Russia's position in the region was extremely weak, both
politically and economically. Although *rapprochement* with China
and diplomatic relations with South Korea had been established by
Soviet President Mikhail Gorbachev, the Soviet Union had not con-

solidated or stabilised its bilateral relationships in the region. Russia also inherited other negative legacies of the Soviet past, such as the long-standing territorial dispute with Japan over the four islands between the Sea of Okhotsk and the North Pacific.

The collapse of the Soviet Union not only affected its constituent republics, but also altered the wider strategic environment and geopolitical structure of North-east Asia. One of the most striking changes was Russia's considerably weakened military position in its Far Eastern regions. Furthermore, radical changes in the country's political and economic systems have altered the domestic factors underpinning its current foreign policy from those of the Soviet period. Ideology and internationalism have been replaced by local interests and nationalism, and the economy has become critical. With the collapse of communism, Russian politics have become more transparent with many new players finding a voice. Among these new players are the authorities and élite of the Russian Far East, which have become an important element of Russia's relations with North-east Asia.

Russia's political and economic problems have tended to restrict both its ability to implement its foreign policy and its role on the international stage. This situation has created a gap between Russia's policy objectives and their actual implementation, or between rhetoric and real policy. This paper examines the shift in the general orientation of Russian foreign policy since 1991 and the implications of this shift for the country's diplomatic relations with North-east Asia. It also assesses the domestic factors and players behind Russia's policy towards the region, and the constraints Moscow faces in implementing that policy. It examines recent developments in Russia's relations with China, Japan and the Korean Peninsula and analyses how these bilateral relationships are changing and what problems they face. The paper concludes with an overall assessment of Russia's current relations with its North-east Asian neighbours, and provides some policy recommendations that, if followed, would enhance regional security overall.

chapter 1

Russia's Place in North-east Asia

Russia's current relations with its North-east Asian neighbours cannot be understood in isolation from Soviet policy towards the region.[1] For the Soviet Union, North-east Asia was an area of secondary concern after Europe and Asia-Pacific countries such as Vietnam and India. Until Mikhail Gorbachev took power in 1985, the Soviet Union had perceived North-east Asia more in terms of threats than opportunities. Policy towards the region in 1964–82 under Leonid Brezhnev had been guided by traditional power consid-erations, focusing almost exclusively on increasing Soviet military might while neglecting the political and economic dimensions of international relations. As a result of this policy, the Soviet Union's geopolitical status in North-east Asia by the mid-1980s was very weak.

Faced with this inheritance, Gorbachev attempted to revise Soviet policy towards the Asia-Pacific region. In a speech in Vladivostok in July 1986, he stressed the importance of the region – and China in particular – for Soviet foreign policy. Gorbachev normalised relations with China in May 1989 and established diplomatic relations with South Korea in September 1990. He could not, however, completely shake off the traditional foreign-policy approach of the Brezhnev era. This legacy, together with Russia's growing economic and political problems, thwarted one of Gorbachev's major policy goals – to ensure a central role for the Soviet Union in the Asia-Pacific, and specifically in North-east Asia.[2]

Accordingly, when the Soviet Union collapsed in December 1991, Russia had to begin its diplomacy with North-east Asia hampered by the politically and economically poor position and relations it had inherited.

This chapter examines the domestic background, interests and constraints behind Russia's policy towards North-east Asia, and identifies the major players involved. It then assesses Russia's policy objectives and the limitations imposed on implementing that policy.

Domestic Politics and the Shift in Foreign Policy

Since 1991, Russians have perceived their country's foreign policy as an extension of its pressing domestic priorities, and have tended to view the external environment through the prism of internal economic and political crises. Russia's domestic politics have thus had a major influence on its foreign policy course.

In the early days of Russia's independence, foreign policy-makers under President Boris Yeltsin and then Foreign Minister Andrei Kozyrev argued that the country's fate was inextricably linked to the West by its commitment to democracy and a market economy, and that Russia's long-term economic development and security depended on close cooperation with the United States, Western Europe and Japan. However, this Western-oriented policy was short lived. From early 1992, this foreign-policy course and Russia's economic reforms had become the object of strident criticism from conservatives and nationalists, particularly in the Supreme Soviet. Since then, there has been a wide-ranging debate in Russia about the basic direction its foreign and security policy should take.[3] This debate not only forms part of an internal power struggle, but also reflects Russia's search for a new identity and national interests. The criticisms levelled against the Yeltsin government were strengthened when nationalist and communist elements dominated the December 1993 elections to the Russian Duma.

In addition to the strong domestic pressure against Yeltsin's Western-oriented foreign policy, the government was experiencing problems with its external relations and realised that it would have to modify its policy orientation. Already disillusioned by poor Western aid for its reform programme, Moscow's disenchantment with and distrust of the West have been strengthened by the progress of NATO enlargement, Russia's marginalisation from international affairs in Europe and Asia, and the difficulties the country is facing in its attempts to integrate into international economic institutions such as the World Trade Organisation and the Paris Club. Furthermore, Western objections to Russia's arms sales – one of its few sources of hard currency – raised Russian suspicions about the West's intentions.[4] As a

moving to an assertive and diversified diplomacy

result, the Yeltsin government soon realised that its national interests often conflicted with those of the West, leading it to shift its foreign-policy emphasis away from its initial Western orientation towards more assertive and diversified diplomacy.[5]

The foreign-policy concept paper drawn up by the Russian Security Council and approved by the President on 23 April 1993 clearly demonstrated this policy shift. It emphasised that Russia should remain and be treated as a 'great power', and declared, for the first time in an official document, that the country's national interests differed from those of the US. The paper listed Russia's relations with foreign countries in the following order of priority:[6]

* the Commonwealth of Independent States (CIS)
* former Eastern Europe
* Western Europe
* the US
* China
* Japan
* the Korean Peninsula
* South and West Asia
* the Middle East
* Central and South America.

This list illustrates Russia's attempt to diversify its foreign relations and its increased interest in North-east Asia – albeit after the CIS, Europe and the US. Interestingly, this list places relations with China above those with Japan.

Defending national interests – with all the connotations this raises of securing great-power status – has become an increasingly prevalent policy goal in Russia. Accordingly, the emphasis on partnership with the West has shifted towards the need to see Russia as an equal.[7] There was also growing recognition among Russia's élite that the country should balance its ties with the West by expanding its links to the East.[8] In his annual message to the Duma in February 1994, President Yeltsin described strengthening Russia's relations with the Asia-Pacific as one of the country's diplomatic tasks for 1994, stating that Russia's geopolitical position as a Eurasian power defined its external relations.[9] Consolidating its relations with North-east Asia, the core of the Asia-Pacific region, and ensuring its influence there, were thus deemed essential elements of Russia's identity as a Eurasian state, one of the bases for its claim to great-power status.

Yet despite the foreign-policy shift away from the West, Foreign Minister Kozyrev was still widely perceived in Russia as being strongly pro-Western, producing a clear divergence between the policy's concept and its actual implementation. In his annual message to the Duma on 23 January 1996, President Yeltsin himself highlighted this discrepancy. The same month, and as a result of the December 1995 Duma elections in which the Communist Party increased its number of seats from 48 to 157, Yeltsin replaced Foreign Minister Kozyrev with Yevgeni Primakov. The new Foreign Minister reaffirmed Russia's policy of establishing an equitable partnership with the West while broadening its international ties away from their excessive Western bias.[10] This was more than mere rhetoric. While maintaining close ties with the US and major West European states, Primakov activated diplomacy towards the CIS, Japan, South Korea, India and parts of Latin America and the Middle East, countries which his predecessor had tended to belittle in his final years as Foreign Minister.

The modification and diversification of Russia's foreign policy was thus motivated by a variety of internal and external factors. However, these factors explain neither the actual interests behind its policy objectives in North-east Asia, nor the constraints affecting the policy's implementation.

Interests and Constraints

The changing security and economic environment of the Russian Far East illustrates both the interests and constraints underlying Russia's foreign and security policy towards North-east Asia.[11]

Map 2 *The Russian Far East*

640 km
1,000 miles

East Siberian Sea

Bering Sea

Anadyr

CHUKOTSKII
AUTONOMOUS OKRUG

KORYAKSKII
AUTONOMOUS
OKRUG

MAGADANSKAYA
OBLAST

REPUBLIC
OF SAKHA

KAMCHATSKAYA
OBLAST

Magadan

Yakutsk

Petropavlovsk-Kamchatskii

KHABAROVSKII

*Sea of
Okhotsk*

SAKHALINSKAYA
OBLAST

EASTERN
SIBERIA

KRAI

R. Amur

AMURSKAYA
OBLAST

Yuzhno-Sakhalinsk

Lake
Baikal

R. Argun

Blagoveshchensk

Khabarovsk

YEVREYSKAYA
AUTONOMOUS OBLAST

PRIMORSKII
KRAI

Ulan Bator

Vladivostok

MONGOLIA

*Sea of
Japan*

JAPAN

NORTH
KOREA

Tokyo

Beijing

Pyongyang

Seoul

CHINA

SOUTH
KOREA

*Yellow
sea*

Shanghai

Administrative division
International boundary
Capital city
Administrative capital

Security

The Russian Far East comprises 6.2 million square kilometres or 36.4% of the total territory of the Russian Federation. Despite its vast size, the region has a sparse population – about 7.6m in 1995 or about 5% of the total Russian population. About half these inhabitants live in the Primorskii (Maritime) and Khabarovskii Krai (29.8% and 20.8% respectively). Russia's Far Eastern region occupies a geopolitically sensitive position close to China, Japan and the Korean Peninsula. Under the communist regime, deteriorating relations with China led to a huge Soviet military build-up in the Russian Far East.[12] *Perestroika* and the collapse of the Union in 1991 drastically changed the region's geopolitics and heralded a continuing reduction in the military forces stationed in the area. The changing security environment was not, however, the only reason for this reduction in Russian forces. More significant has been the country's economic crisis, which has forced cuts in the military, both quantitative and qualitative.

In February 1997, then Minister of Defence Igor Rodionov publicly stated that Russia's protracted economic crisis threatened to reduce the armed forces to nothing by 2003, and that even the strategic nuclear forces were in a state of near-total collapse.[13] Although Rodionov made these remarks to focus public attention on the crisis in an attempt to obtain more funds for the military, it was still an unusual outburst for a Minister of Defence. Russia's military in its Far East, although still a large-scale force with a nuclear element, has been steadily reduced in size (see Table 1, pp. 20–21). In qualitative terms, too, it faces a wide range of problems common to the Russian military as a whole, including delays in receiving wages, low morale, housing and food shortages, poor discipline and the illegal diversion of weapons. The level of military activity in the region including training, has consequently been extremely low.[14]

military activity has been extremely low

How does the leadership in Moscow see the current security environment surrounding its country? Russia is in a politically and strategically defensive position on its western borders, particularly in response to NATO enlargement, while it is in an unstable and vulnerable position on its southern borders with the CIS. To the east, despite its weakened military but with no immediate military threat and with no border changes created by the collapse of the Soviet Union, Russia is in a relatively stable geopolitical position and is less immediately concerned about its own security. Nevertheless, it is sensitive about the security of the eastern borders it shares with states such as China, with its growing economic and military power and uncertain future; Japan, with its US military presence and unresolved territorial dispute with Russia; and the Korean Peninsula, with its tensions and unpredictable future status.

Moscow's other security concerns relate to demographic changes in the Russian Far East. The region's population decreased from 8m in 1992 to 7.6m in 1995. Yet it also attracts large numbers of illegal Chinese immigrants about whom there are no official data. These trends have caused concern in Russia, and some observers point out that the region's 'demographic vacuum' could become a destabilising factor for the balance of power in North-east Asia.[15] However, given the overall security environment and Russia's severely limited financial resources, some analysts forecast that the Russian military presence in the Far Eastern region is likely to decline further, both quantitatively and qualitatively, although capable nuclear forces are likely to be retained.[16] This trend requires Russia to improve its security environment in North-east Asia, which currently lacks a multilateral security system. This could be done, for example, through arms-reduction measures on the Sino-Russian borders, or by building up bilateral confidence-building measures (CBMs), which would allow the Russian military to continue to downsize while minimising the impact of this reduction on Russia's strategic place in the region.[17] But, as Russia's strategic status in the region may deteriorate still further, its long-term security objective is to create a multilateral regional security system that would allow it to remain involved in regional security at a low cost.[18]

The only existing bilateral security regime in the region is dominated by the US, and Russia has mixed feelings about the US military presence in North-east Asia. While Moscow acknowledges that the US role guarantees stability, it is also frustrated by the US predominance. However, Russia has not strongly pushed the concept of a multilateral security system. In 1994, then Foreign Minister Kozyrev described the creation of a 'Security Association'

Table 1 *Soviet/Russian Forces in the Far Eastern Military District*

	1989–90	1990–91	1991–92
Ground forces			
Tank divisions	3	3	3
Motor rifle divisions	21	18	18
Pacific Fleet			
Submarines	120	110	98
SSBN*	24	24	24
Principal surface combatants	77	69	63
Carriers	2	2	2
Cruisers	11	15	14
Destroyers	8	7	7
Frigates	56	45	40

*nuclear-fuelled ballistic-missile submarines

Source International Institute for Strategic Studies, *The Military Balance*, 1987–97

as a long-term goal, at the same time adding that Russia had no illusions about its immediate feasibility, but that the region should gradually move in this direction.[19]

In general terms, military might still carries weight in power politics. Military strength was the major source of Soviet influence in the Asia-Pacific region, although the Soviet Union failed to translate this into effective political influence. Russia's dwindling military presence in its Far East shows a further loss of credible political power, and has weakened the country's geostrategic position in North-east Asia relative to its neighbours, which could affect the implementation of its regional foreign policy.

Economics
During the Soviet era, Russian Far East trade centred on exporting raw materials to the Soviet republics and its satellite states in Eastern Europe. In return, the Russian Far East depended on imports from other regions for its consumer goods. Soviet leaders, including Gorbachev, spoke of restructuring the region's economy to make better use of its potential, especially in manufacturing its natural

1992–93	1993–94	1994–95	1995–96	1996–97
3	3	3	3	0
16	16	16	13	10
86	66	51	51	43
21	20	16	18	14
54	49	50	49	45
1	0	0	0	0
13	14	9	9	4
7	7	6	6	7
33	28	35	34	34

resources. Although several special programmes to develop the economy were drawn up, they remained mere rhetoric and were never actually put into practice. Historically, Moscow has seemed only distantly concerned with events east of Lake Baikal. Since the collapse of the Soviet Union, the structure of the Russian Far Eastern economy has exacerbated the region's economic crisis caused by Russia's transformation from a centrally planned to a market economy.

The decline of the military–industrial complex was particularly problematic for the region whose economy had been so dependent on military personnel and military–industrial production during the Soviet era. The loss of financial support from the federal government in Moscow for these Soviet-era industries meant that uncompetitive industries were no longer eligible for the subsidies that had previously allowed them to exist. The cost of fuel and electric power in the region is also much higher than Russia's average. Furthermore, poor transport infrastructure has caused enormous problems, particularly for the Russian Far East, which depends on exporting its resources to distant regions further west in

Table 2 *Russian Trade with the US and North-east Asia*

(US$m, %)	1994			1995		
	Export	Import	Total	Export	Import	Total
World total	62,937	38,545	101,482	77,398	46,359	123,757
	100.0	100.0	100.0	100.0	100.0	100.0
US	3,748	2,071	5,819	5,092	2,651	7,743
	6.0	5.4	5.7	6.6	5.7	6.3
China	2,838	952	3,790	3,377	865	4,242
	4.5	2.5	3.7	4.4	1.9	3.4
Japan	2,267	1,114	3,381	3,173	763	3,936
	3.6	2.9	3.3	4.1	1.6	3.2
South Korea	370	429	799	747	502	1,249
	0.6	1.1	0.8	1.0	1.1	1.0
Taiwan	194	137	331	463	88	551
	0.3	0.4	0.3	0.6	0.2	0.4
North Korea	52	44	96	70	15	85
	0.08	0.11	0.09	0.09	0.03	0.07

Source *Direction of Trade Statistics Yearbook* (Washington DC: International Monetary Fund, 1996)

Table 3 *Distribution of Russian Trade*

(%)	1994			1995		
	Export	Import	Total	Export	Import	Total
World Total	100.0	100.0	100.0	100.0	100.0	100.0
Industrial Countries	51.9	51.2	51.6	49.7	49.1	49.5
Europe	35.6	38.4	36.6	34.4	41.5	37.1
Developing Countries	47.6	47.9	47.7	49.9	50.4	50.1
Western Hemisphere	1.3	1.3	1.3	2.7	1.9	2.6
Asia	8.4	6.9	7.9	10.3	5.9	8.6
Middle East	2.0	0.9	1.6	2.1	0.9	1.6
Africa	0.3	0.3	0.3	0.4	0.3	0.3
Others	0.5	0.9	0.7	0.4	0.5	0.4

Source *Ibid.*

return for imports of consumer goods. To make matters worse, Moscow increased railway charges, which threatened to deprive the Far Eastern industries of their traditional markets in European Russia and the CIS, and, in general, has separated the Far Eastern region economically from the rest of Russia west of the Urals.

As a result, the Far East has turned to external economic relations. Purchases of food and other consumer goods from Russia's western regions declined dramatically from 1992–94. Already in 1992, the Russian Far East received no less than 30% of all its consumer goods from abroad.[20] In 1995, nearly half the region's imports from abroad were food and consumer goods (see Table 7, p. 26). In 1995, Russia's trade turnover with China, Japan and South Korea amounted to $9.4 billion – a mere 7.6% of its total trade. In the same year, the total trade turnover of the Russian Far East region was about $4.2bn, of which trade with the three North-east Asian powers amounted to $2.3bn. The major traders in the Russian Far East were Primorskii Krai (accounting for $1.25bn or 30% of the region's total trade), Khabarovskii Krai ($0.85bn, 20%) and Sakhalin-skaya Oblast ($0.77bn, 18%). Their major trade partners were Japan ($1.36bn, 33%), the US ($0.6bn, 14%), South Korea ($0.47bn, 11%) and China ($0.33bn, 8%), and the total trade of these three districts added up to more than two-thirds of the region's total trade (see Tables 2–7). These statistics demonstrate that although Russia's trade relations with North-east Asia are still weak, those of its Far Eastern region are relatively strong, particularly in the border regions.

Although increasing investment is vital for the Russian Far East, there are many obstacles to foreign and domestic investment. Russia has not yet developed a coherent legal framework with transparent rules for domestic and foreign investment or joint ventures. Duties levied against importers have been regularly increased leading to rampant corruption, custom rules are applied inconsistently. The Russian *mafya*'s control of business, difficulties in obtaining accurate business information, and poor transport and other infrastructure are also powerful obstacles to investment.[21]

obstacles to foreign and domestic investment

The economic crisis has also caused socioeconomic problems in the region, the negative effects of which could easily spill over the

Table 4 *Russian Far East Trade*

(US$m, %)	1994			1995		
	Export	Import	Total	Export	Import	Total
Total	1,610.5	649.3	2,259.8	2,426.8	1,753.4	4,180.2
	100.0	100.0	100.0	100.0	100.0	100.0
Primorskii Krai						
	435.0	156.0	591.0	637.9	612.0	1,249.9
	27.0	24.0	26.2	26.3	34.9	29.9
Khabarovskii Krai						
	403.1	130.2	533.3	559.7	288.7	848.4
	25.0	20.0	23.6	23.1	16.5	20.3
Sakhalinskaya Oblast						
	219.4	43.9	263.3	490.0	280.0	770.0
	13.6	6.8	11.7	20.2	16.0	18.4
Kamchatskaya Oblast						
	288.0	85.0	373.0	393.3	147.1	540.4
	17.9	13.1	16.5	16.2	8.4	12.9
Republic of Sakha						
	171.8	132.3	304.1	244.1	220.8	464.9
	10.7	20.4	13.5	10.1	12.6	11.1
Magadanskaya Oblast						
	13.9	59.6	73.5	30.0	122.4	152.4
	0.9	9.2	3.3	1.2	7.0	3.6
Amurskaya Oblast						
	69.1	36.6	105.7	63.8	76.3	140.1
	4.3	5.6	4.7	2.6	4.4	3.4
Yevreyskaya Autonomous Oblast						
	10.2	6.2	16.4	8.0	6.1	14.1
	0.6	1.0	0.7	0.3	0.3	0.3

Source Japan External Trade Organisation, *Eastern Europe Newsletter*, July 1996

borders. In 1994, the crime rate in the Russian Far East was about 35% higher than Russia's average. Environmental issues have already caused diplomatic problems, for example, with Japan over Russia's dumping of nuclear waste in the Sea of Japan in October 1993, and the serious contamination of the Sea from an oil leak caused by a sunk Russian tanker in January 1997.

Table 5 *Russian Far East Trade Partners*

(US$m, %)	1994			1995		
	Export	Import	Total	Export	Import	Total
Total	1,605.1	649.8	2,254.9	2,426.8	1,753.4	4,180.2
	100.0	100.0	100.0	100.0	100.0	100.0
Japan	995.0	110.1	1,105.1	1,173.3	188	1,361.3
	62	16.9	49.0	48.3	10.7	32.6
US	63.6	112.4	176	220.9	376.3	597.2
	4.0	17.3	7.8	9.1	21.5	14.3
South Korea	163.3	98.6	261.9	253.5	212.2	465.7
	10.2	15.2	11.6	10.5	12.1	11.1
China	156.0	94.6	250.6	172.4	155.6	328.0
	9.7	14.6	11.1	7.1	8.9	7.9
Germany	19.3	17.4	36.7	50.4	198.6	249.0
	1.2	2.7	1.6	2.1	11.3	6.0
Vietnam	7.2	10.5	17.7	147.7	23.4	171.1
	0.4	1.6	0.8	6.1	1.3	4.1
Singapore	25.7	14.5	40.2	36.7	42.1	78.8
	1.6	2.2	1.8	1.5	2.4	1.9
Switzerland	15.5	19.7	35.2	39.8	8.6	48.4
	1.0	3.0	1.6	1.6	0.5	1.2
Canada	19.1	19.2	38.3	33.1	11.8	44.9
	1.2	3.0	1.7	1.4	0.7	1.1
Australia	31.1	7.7	38.8	2.2	31.7	33.9
	1.9	1.2	1.7	0.1	1.8	0.8
CIS	n.a.	n.a.	n.a.	26.0	138.6	164.6
	n.a.	n.a.	n.a.	1.1	7.9	3.9
Others	109.3	145.1	254.4	271.8	365.5	637.3
	6.8	22.3	11.3	11.2	20.8	15.2

Source *Ibid.*

In May 1996, President Yeltsin signed a special long-term programme for the economic development of the Transbaikal and Russian Far East regions. The programme's aim was to make better use of these regions' rich natural resources and valuable geo-economic position. Integral to the project is a special sub-programme designed to stimulate business cooperation between the Russian Far

Table 6 *Russian Far East Exports*
(US$m, %)

	1994		1995	
Total	1,610.5	100.0	2,426.8	100.0
Food products	704.0	43.7	1,132.0	46.6
Fuel, minerals, metals	464.0	28.8	548.7	22.6
Raw materials and unfinished goods	317.2	19.7	417.2	17.2
Machinery and transportation equipment	32.0	2.0	185.9	7.7
Chemical products	19.8	1.2	35.7	1.5
Construction materials	4.3	0.3	1.7	0.1
Consumer goods	3.1	0.2	2.5	0.1
Other	66.1	4.1	103.2	4.3

Source *Ibid.*

Table 7 *Russian Far East Imports*
(US$m, %)

	1994		1995	
Total	649.8	100.0	1,753.4	100.0
Consumer goods	319.2	49.1	810.7	46.2
Food, beverages	144.7	22.3	340.7	19.4
Other	174.4	26.8	470.0	26.8
Machinery and transportation equipment	210.4	32.4	518.4	29.6
Fuel, minerals, metals	36.0	5.5	42.3	2.4
Chemical products	22.2	3.4	25.8	1.5
Construction materials	9.2	1.4	13.0	0.7
Raw materials and unfinished goods	0.9	0.1	8.7	0.5
Other	51.9	8.0	334.5	19.1

Source *Ibid.*

East and Eastern Siberia and their Asia-Pacific neighbours. To this end, the programme would give these regions a certain level of economic autonomy. The programme also invites foreign capital to invest in regional projects. Although the programme has been finalised, what concrete measures Moscow will really take to implement it have yet to be seen. The estimated total budget for the project is about 370 trillion roubles over the next two decades, of which the central government will provide 25% and local governments and private enterprises 50%, with the balance coming from foreign sources. However, given Russia's budgetary constraints and domestic balance of power, it is too optimistic to expect wholesale budgetary redistribution among Russia's regions. Indeed, in the 1997 government budget, only 3% of the development programme's projected budget was appropriated. This is a clear example of the gap between Moscow's rhetoric and its real policy.

The rich natural resources of Siberia and the Russian Far East will remain the bedrock of Russia's place in the world economy and could provide it with diplomatic leverage in the future. But exploiting these resources, especially the oil and gas reserves, requires huge capital investment which Russia simply cannot afford. Instead, it hopes that the development programme will help to channel foreign resources into the region. Russia sees Japan and South Korea as clear candidates for financial investment, and China as a candidate for other forms of economic cooperation, such as labour.

These economic imperatives thus underpin Russia's policy towards these countries as well as its goal of integrating its Far Eastern economy into those of the Asia-Pacific. At the same time, Russia's economic difficulties and the various obstacles to the economic development of its Far East could constrain the implementation of this policy.

Players and Constituencies

Today, Russian politics remains a mainly élite game, played by competing government organisations and the leaders of state-affiliated corporate groups. It is, however, opening up and more players are joining the field. These newcomers now include regional leaders and élite groups who often attempt to assert their own interests over those of Moscow. The role of these leaders and élites in the Russian Far East has a particular bearing on Russia's relations with North-east Asia, and the interplay between localism, nationalism and regionalism is likely to be a major theme of political relations between the Russian Far East and North-east Asia in the long term.[22]

Regional Leaders

Power relations between Moscow and the regions have changed dramatically since the collapse of the Soviet Union. Central control over the regions began deteriorating even before the Soviet Union disintegrated. Although legislative distinctions had little political significance while the Soviet Union survived, after its collapse they took on new importance. Resentment over disparities in economic rights among regional entities was exacerbated by the government's failure to fulfil some of the promises President Yeltsin had made to regional leaders during his political struggle with Gorbachev in late 1991, guaranteeing them a larger percentage of the profits from the sale of resources on their territories.[23] The nationalist- and communist-dominated results of the Duma elections in December 1993 and 1995 suggested that much of the Russian Far East, especially Primorskii Krai and Sakhalinskaya Oblast, is becoming more nationalistic. The number of votes obtained by Vladimir Zhirinovsky's Liberal Democratic Party (LDP) in Primorskii Krai, Sakhalinskaya Oblast and some other parts of the Far East was much higher than the average in Russia as a whole. For example, in Primorskii Krai, the LDP received 23.3% of the national vote in December 1993 and 20.5% in December 1995, while the average in Russia as a whole was 22.9% and 11.2% respectively.[24]

Regional dissatisfaction with the relationship with Moscow and the urgent need to pursue a development policy compatible with local realities has helped to encourage Russian Far Eastern localism and regionalism. The region's local élite has attempted to gain new functions and concessions from Moscow. Opportunities for increased autonomy in economic decision-making have led the regions to formulate their own foreign

Far Eastern localism and regionalism

economic policies, or to assert political claims in their foreign relations. The Association of the Far East and Za-Baikal Regional Economic Cooperation was set up by the Far Eastern Krais and Oblasts in 1990 to coordinate economic and social development, and to take a unified stand towards Moscow. However, the Association is still weak and has difficulty adopting a unified position on specific issues as a result of the regions' different economic structures and interests, and of rivalry among their governors.[25] The Association also promotes non-governmental regional cooperation and exchanges between the Russian Far East and North-east Asia. It organises and coordinates the annual North-east Asian Governors' Conference, the annual Russian–Japanese Far Eastern Governors' Conference and various other regional economic committees with Japan, China, South and North Korea and the US.

Reflecting their respective geopolitical positions, the governors of Primorskii Krai, Khabarovskii Krai and Sakhalinskaya Oblast have regularly spoken not only on regional economic issues, but also on the political issue of bilateral relations with neighbouring countries. They strongly oppose making any concessions to Japan on the territorial dispute or to China on border issues. In February 1995, the regional legislature of Primorskii Krai voted to cease all operations to demarcate the eastern part of the Sino-Russian border and to create its own commission to negotiate with China. Governor Yevgeny Nazdrachenko not only supported this decision, but repeatedly declared his intention to work to rescind the 1991 Soviet–Chinese treaty on boundary demarcation.[26] Nazdrachenko's public opposition to this treaty provoked a strong reaction from Moscow, and President Yeltsin ordered Nazdrachenko to coordinate all his statements on Sino-Russian relations with the Russian Foreign Ministry.[27] In November 1996, the Governor of Khabarovskii Krai, Viktor Ishaev, pubicly announced that the Krai had violated the treaty by decreeing that ships navigating in the Amur River close to Khabarovsk required permission from the local authorities. According to the treaty, such shipping only requires notification, not written permission.[28]

The substantial number of legal and illegal Chinese immigrants in the Russian Far East, particularly in Primorskii and Khabarovskii Krai, has created social and political upheavals at the local level, intensifying the concerns of both the regional authorities and the public.[29]

The governors of Primorskii and Khabarovskii Krai and Sakhalinskaya Oblast, as seen above, tend to argue against or actively oppose Moscow's foreign policy, presumably because of their regional political interests, and in an attempt to force central government to compromise. The influence of these governors on relations with neighbouring countries has so far been limited, although it is likely to grow in future. On the whole, the powers and responsibilities of the regional authorities and their ability to influence local social and economic affairs have been substantially increased since the collapse of the Soviet Union as part of Moscow's bid to decentralise administration. Furthermore, since 1996 all governors are elected by their constituencies instead of being appointed by the President as was previously the case, and thus have to make every effort to represent and realise local interests to increase their chances of winning the next elections. The demand for more autonomous rights to resources and economic policy will therefore continue to rise. In certain cases, the regions will attempt to increase their influence in their relations with neighbouring countries, or even approach outside governments directly for economic links.

In addition, the governors of the Far Eastern regions are deputies of the Upper House of the Russian parliament, they have a legitimate channel through which to present their claims to, and exert political pressure on, Moscow. Furthermore, since regional leaders are likely to have increasing influence on the outcome of presidential elections in their constituency, the President and his government will have to pay much more attention to their demands than they have thus far. Given the constraints Russia's political, economic and security circumstances impose on policy implementation, and the increased demands of regional leaders based on their local interests, central government is likely to have greater difficulty in formulating and implementing policy towards Northeast Asia in future.

Military Leaders
Russia's military leaders have privileged access to the President and a key voice on security matters, and have had a selective and often

indirect impact on foreign policy. The view that Russia is a great power is more prevalent among the military than among other élite groups. Not surprisingly, politicians have vied for the support, tacit or explicit, of military commanders, especially during periods of serious political discord.[30]

While the Russian Foreign Ministry in the immediate post-Soviet period tended to favour negotiations on the territorial dispute with Japan, Russian military leaders and regional commanders took a more cautious or negative view, arguing that the islands were key for Russia's Far Eastern defence. This military position has been consistent since the Soviet era, and despite the geostrategic changes after 1991 and the need to reduce the size of the Russian military in the Far East, there is no evidence that this view has changed. Although the Russian military's influence on Russian–Japanese relations as a whole is limited, the territorial issue occupies such an important place in bilateral relations that the military will continue to play an important part in policy-making. This could restrict the Foreign Ministry's manoeuvrability and flexibility.

The Russian military appears to take a less clear-cut line on China. While some see it as a potential threat, others argue that China could be used as a political bargaining tool in relations with the West, particularly the US. In any event, given Russia's weakened military stature, military leaders – including local commanders in the Far East – are likely to consent to troop reductions along the borders with China and to develop confidence-building measures with all neighbouring countries.

Economic Groups

The Yeltsin administration depends heavily on the support of sympathetic economic groups – so much so that it would have difficulty refusing requests for special consideration of foreign trade policy. At the same time, it must be careful not to exaggerate the policy impact of lobbying by economic groups, particularly in external strategic policy terms. As far as relations with North-east Asia are concerned, Russia's defence and energy industries are the most relevant economic groups.

The defence industry

Following the end of the Cold War, there was a clear decline in

Russia's arms trade. The country now accounts for 6–10% of all reported international arms transfers, while the Soviet Union regularly accounted for at least one-third of the world market.[31] Since 1992, Russia's defence procurement has declined by around two-thirds in value terms compared to average Soviet levels.[32] Arms sales are still one of Russia's few major sources of hard currency. By increasing its arms sales, the Russian government also expects to stabilise the rapid decline in its defence–industrial sector, minimise unemployment, finance defence conversion, and promote greater social and economic order.

Central government in conjunction with the defence industries, has been attempting to rebuild the arms trade through diplomatic means and to put it on a firm commercial basis. Defence industries exert a strong political influence on central government. Among others, the state-owned Rosvooruzhenie company represents the industry's interests in Moscow.[33] Since the major industries in many Far Eastern cities are defence-related and are

Table 8 *Russian Arms Deliveries, cumulative value 1992–1994*

	US$m	%
Total	6,550	100
East Asia	1,855	28.3
China	1,700	26.0
Vietnam	90	1.4
North Korea	50	0.8
Laos	10	0.2
South Korea	5	0.1
Middle East	1,590	24.3
Europe	1,205	18.4
South Asia	940	14.4
India	925	14.1
Africa	610	9.3
Americas	255	3.9
Central Asia and the Caucasus	95	1.5

Source *World Military Expenditures and Arms Transfers* (Washington DC: US Arms Control and Disarmament Agency, 1995)

now severely affected by cutbacks in military spending, the incentives to sell arms and ammunition abroad is especially strong in the Russian Far East. The military–industrial complex is thus most likely to lobby to promote arms sale to the Asia-Pacific region, especially to China, a key arms market for Russia. In 1994, Moscow agreed with Seoul that it would repay its debt to South Korea with arms (see Chapter 4 below). Russia has resumed its large-scale arms trade with China, worth over $2.5bn in 1992–95.[34] China has already become the largest recipient of Russia's arms receiving more than a quarter of its total arms deliveries, cumulative 1992–94 (see Table 8).

Although data on the benefits the military–industrial complex in the Russian Far East receives from the arms trade are not available, the Gagarin aircraft industrial complex in Khabarovskii Krai, for example, produces Su-27 fighter aircraft, of which more than 30 have already been delivered to China at a lucrative profit (see Chapter 2 below). The Gagarin aircraft industrial complex undoubtedly received large profits from this sale.

As some observers point out, the initiative for selling China the latest, fully equipped Su-27 and the means to produce its own version of the plane reportedly came from the manufacturer. Despite official justification, the proliferation of decision-makers and actors and lack of effective coordination fragment policy and make it difficult to ascertain Russia's real intentions in selling arms to China. Are these sales based on careful strategic considerations of Russia's internal and regional security, or are they simply based on commercial considerations?[35] The stakes are high since arms sales to China could affect the regional balance of power and security.

The energy industry

The oil and gas industries, and the energy sector more generally, are the most prominent business groups to have become involved in domestic and foreign policy. The energy sector's key economic role in Russian exports – oil and gas account for the bulk of foreign-exchange earnings – gives it an enormous stake in, and considerable influence over, external economic policy. Large oil and gas enterprises are closely associated with the government, and Gazprom, the largest gas enterprise, has direct links to political leaders including Prime Minister Viktor Chernomyrdin. This combination of economic weight and political access has given the energy sector the most important place among economic lobby groups.[36]

This sector has a strong interest in promoting the supply of gas and oil to China, Japan and South Korea from Siberia and Sakhalinskaya Oblast, and in attracting foreign investment to explore energy resources. Russia's Ministry for the Fuel and Power Industry is shifting the focus of its foreign economic activity eastwards because the Russian Far East, and Sakhalinskaya Oblast in particular, contains vast reserves offering unprecedented export prospects. The Ministry regards the Sakhalin-1 and Sakhalin-2 projects to exploit oil and natural gas off the coast of Sakhalin, for which production-sharing agreements were signed in 1995 and 1994 respectively with both Japanese and US companies, as the first stage in attracting major foreign investment for the long-term exploration of Far Eastern and East Siberian deposits. The Ministry is also working on other projects with China and South Korea, including constructing a gas pipeline to South Korea via Mongolia and China, and an oil pipeline to China with probable access to the Pacific coast which could deliver oil to any Asian country.[37]

the energy sector is the most powerful lobby

Russia's energy sector as a whole could promote a favourable investment environment for developing its resources in the Russian Far East that would establish economic cooperation with North-east Asian countries. However, as examined above, Russia's economic crisis may well inhibit these aspirations.

Combining Interests, Constraints and Players

Russia's current political, economic and military difficulties have curtailed its state power, prevented the full implementation of its foreign and security policy, and obscured its international role. Furthermore, the proliferation of decision-makers and political players, coupled with a lack of coherent policy coordination, has made it difficult for both Russians and external analysts to identify the precise direction of the country's economic and foreign policies.[38] Political rhetoric must be carefully analysed and distinguished from real policy, and policy objectives must be differentiated from their actual implementation.

The country's internal politics have had a major influence on the shift in orientation of its foreign policy, and have driven the Yeltsin government to initiate active diplomacy to ensure Russia's influence as a Eurasian state in the Asia-Pacific, and above all in North-east Asia. The shift in emphasis towards the Asia-Pacific was also partly a reaction against Russia's earlier Western-oriented policy. In this sense, Russia's relations with the West and with North-east Asia are interlinked. Trends in Russia's foreign policy also demonstrate that despite the public rhetoric of the Yeltsin administration, its real policy still attaches primary importance to relations with the West. But a change in both the leadership and the domestic political environment could easily affect the current policy course. This would be felt directly not only in Europe, but also in Asia. With the growing localism and regionalism of the Russian Far East, the influence of its leaders on relations with North-east Asia – particularly leaders in Primorskii and Khabarovskii Krai and Sakhalinskaya Oblast – is likely to strengthen in the future. As a result, Moscow is likely to find formulating and implementing policy towards North-east Asia a much more complicated and occasionally difficult process than hitherto, which could widen the gap between its rhetoric and real policy still further. This also implies that not only Russian policy-makers, but also their North-east Asian foreign-policy counterparts would have to pay much more attention to the Russian Far East region in their policy-making.

Although Russia's domestic situation and interests dictate that it should play an influential role in North-east Asia, its current weak political and economic ties with the region and the negative legacy of the Soviet past will prevent it doing so in the short term. To offset the negative effect of the financial crisis on its military force levels in its Far Eastern region, Russia must help to foster a stable and favourable security environment in North-east Asia by strengthening its bilateral political and security relations.

To become an Asia-Pacific power, Russia must increase its economic interdependence – first and foremost that of its Far East – with the economies of its North-east Asian neighbours.[39] However, various obstacles stand in the way of this process. Russia's domestic interests and needs have also driven it to improve its trade relations with North-east Asia in an attempt to increase economic cooperation for developing its Far East. This desire for economic integration has motivated it to seek membership in the Asia-Pacific Economic Cooperation (APEC) process. But Russia's domestic economic crisis, the obstacles hindering the development of its Far Eastern economy, and poor trade links with North-east Asia have made implementing these policies difficult.

chapter 2

China

China has come to play a major role in both the rhetoric and substance of Russia's foreign policy, and to occupy the central place in its relations with North-east Asia.

China was not an important element in the Yeltsin government's early foreign policy. Following the collapse of the Soviet regime, the new Western-oriented leadership in Moscow had no reason to develop a close relationship with communist China. But as Russia's foreign policy shifted away from the West, it placed greater emphasis on relations with China as a major Eastern power. The government in Beijing, for its part, was concerned about the possible impact the Soviet Union's collapse would have on China. Indeed, Russia's economic crisis convinced many in China that their own course of economic reform was the best path to follow. But there was an additional strategic aspect to China's concerns about the new regime in Russia. The Yeltsin government's initial stance had clearly demonstrated its intention to 'Westernise' Russia and make it an integral part or even ally of the West. Had this course of action been pursued, it would have tipped the global balance of power against China and Chinese socialism. But these initial concerns were quickly assuaged and China naturally saw Russia's shift away from its Western-oriented foreign policy as a positive development.

There are now clear reasons for Russia to improve its relations with China, and to emphasise aspects of its China policy. Above all, security issues – such as safeguarding the long Sino-Russian borders

– have driven Moscow to improve bilateral relations, which is also in China's security interest. Both governments wish to reduce tension along their common borders, for example by reducing the size of their forces stationed along the borders and by introducing CBMs. Bilateral arms-reduction measures and CBMs could also help to create a favourable environment for a future multilateral security system in North-east Asia, which is Russia's long-term objective. By reducing the threat potential along the Sino-Russian border, China could secure for itself a much stronger geostrategic and geopolitical position from which to proceed with its economic reform programme, assert its interests in the Asia-Pacific region, and face the US on which China used to depend strategically in the face of the Soviet military threat.

Economics – above all the arms trade – has also brought Russia and China closer together. At a time when its military–industrial complex has been severely reduced by the move to a market economy, Russia's arms sale to China have become an essential source of revenue. China, in turn, needs to acquire modern weapons and advanced military technology at low prices to counter arms sale to Taiwan by the US and Western Europe. As a result, China has become the number one market for Russian arms.[1] China is also one of the few countries to have shown an interest in Russian industrial goods and technology. China is Russia's main export market for finished industrial goods, and various Chinese industries benefit from Russian technology transfers. In turn, Russia represents an important market for China's surplus consumer goods. In particular, it exports large quantities of inexpensive commodities to Siberia and the Russian Far East which have depended on foreign consumer goods since the changes that followed the collapse of communism in 1991.

Over time, the US has become an important factor in Sino-Russian relations. While Russia and China accord high priority to their relationship with the US, both countries also resent what they see as US attempts to force its policy objectives onto them and to exert excessive pressure in such areas as arms sales and technology transfers. In addition, Russia considers that its security is threatened by NATO enlargement eastwards, while China objects to US pressure on its human-rights record, trade policies and the Taiwan issue. Some Chinese scholars believe that new tensions have developed between major powers because of US power politics, and that Washington is seeking to reinforce its military alliance in the Asia-Pacific in an attempt to contain both Russia and China.[2] Although this is not the official view of the government in Beijing, it is a widely held Chinese opinion of the US.

The Start of a New Relationship

President Yeltsin visited China from 17–19 December 1992, the first visit by a Russian President. This was heralded as the start of a new era in Sino-Russian relations, characterised by close military and economic cooperation. On 18 December, Yeltsin and Chinese President Jiang Zemin signed the Joint Declaration of the Russian Federation and the People's Republic of China on the Basic Principles Governing their Bilateral Relations. In addition, the two Presidents signed some 12 other agreements, including plans for China to participate in developing the natural resources of Siberia and the Russian Far East, the projected construction of a nuclear reactor in China, and other forms of scientific and technical cooperation.

Military cooperation figured prominently in talks between the two leaders. Yeltsin welcomed the opportunity of selling arms to China, noting that China had purchased $1.8bn-worth of weapons and parts from Russia in 1992 – 24 Su-27 jet fighters plus S-300 air-defence missile systems. The two sides also agreed to accelerate joint negotiations on border issues – together with Kazakstan, Kyrgyzstan and Tajikistan – in an attempt to reach a settlement on China's disputed western borders. In addition, Yeltsin and Zemin consented to establish a zone of stability in the border areas, restricting military forces, installations and activity to a depth of 100km along the frontier. The precise details were left to be agreed in later negotiations.

President Jiang Zemin made a return visit to Russia on 2–6 September 1994. On 3 September, the two Presidents signed the Sino-Russian Joint Declaration which termed their bilateral relationship a 'constructive partnership'. It also stated that Russia and China were major powers in the 'multipolar world system', and included a general agreement to reduce the number of border troops further. The same day, the two Presidents also signed the Joint Statement of the Presidents of the Russian Federation and the People's Republic of China in which they agreed not to target strategic nuclear weapons at – or use nuclear weapons against – each other. Additional agreements were reached to increase military cooperation, construct a Russian nuclear-power station in North-eastern China, and for Russia to assist China in building several major industrial facilities.

The Sino-Russian 'Strategic Partnership'

President Yeltsin made his second visit to Beijing on 24–27 April 1996, not quite two months before the Russian presidential elections in June. The two Presidents signed a Sino-Russian Joint Statement on 25 April.[3] This visit and the Joint Statement are good illustrations of certain aspects, both rhetorical and substantive, of the current Sino-Russian relationship. Yeltsin and Jiang declared in their Joint Statement that they would develop a 'strategic partnership', a phrase that replaced the 'constructive partnership' of the September 1994 Joint Declaration. The official explanation given by both sides was that the term 'strategic partnership' confirmed their mutual political will to strengthen cooperation in various fields, and there is clearly some strategic significance in such major powers as Russia and China establishing a constructive partnership, but pursuing broad common interests and close cooperation is not the same as creating a formal alliance. Indeed, the substance of Sino-Russian bilateral relations gives no indication that 'strategic partnership' means 'alliance'. Is, then, the term 'strategic partnership' simply a rhetorical device, or does it have an overtly political meaning?

'strategic partnership' does not mean 'alliance'

The domestic political atmosphere in Russia before Yeltsin's second visit to China in 1996 was characterised by growing anti-Western feeling, triggered above all by NATO's bombardment of Serb forces in the former Yugoslavia in August 1995. Other significant events included the communist and nationalist victories in the December 1993 and 1995 Duma elections; the progress of NATO enlargement, a central issue for Russia's political élite; and the fact that Yeltsin was to contest the presidential elections just two months after his visit to China. Against this background, Yeltsin had to demonstrate to his domestic audience that his visit had been successful and had resulted in closer ties with China. Yeltsin's visit also came just after tension between Beijing and Washington had risen dramatically when China conducted a series of military exercises in waters off Taiwan in March 1996. The US responded by despatching two carrier battlegroups to the Taiwan Strait. Given this US show of military strength and NATO enlargement eastwards, both Beijing and Moscow had an interest in sending a strong message to the West, particularly the US, by demonstrating their closer bilateral relations.

According to the official press briefing following the summit, President Jiang expressed his understanding and support for Russia's position on NATO enlargement, and stated that expanding the Atlantic Alliance went against the current of the times. In the Joint Statement, both leaders expressed their support for each other on sensitive domestic issues such as Chechnya, Taiwan and Tibet, which have all prompted an international reaction. On Taiwan, the Statement asserted:

> *The Russian Federation reiterates that the government of the People's Republic of China is the sole legal government representing the whole of China, and Taiwan is an inalienable part of the Chinese territory. Russia will not establish official relations nor enter into official contacts with Taiwan.*

In its relations with Taiwan, Russia has attempted a delicate balancing act of increasing economic and cultural ties without antagonising Beijing. In September 1992, Yeltsin had issued a decree reassuring China that Russia would avoid formal political relations with Taiwan. Although Russian trade with Taiwan increased from $213m in 1992 to $551m in 1995, it still accounted for less than one-seventh of its total trade with China.

Aside from the rhetoric and political declarations, Yeltsin's visit also had a concrete effect on security. On 26 April 1996 in Shanghai, the Presidents of China, Russia, Kazakstan, Kyrgyzstan and Tajikistan signed an Agreement on Military Confidence-building in the Border Areas. This Agreement included exchanging information about the military forces deployed in these areas, notification of exercises near the borders, limiting the scale of these exercises, and establishing mutual inspections. The Russian and Chinese Presidents agreed to continue negotiations to reduce their military forces in the border areas. As a result of these negotiations, the five Presidents signed an agreement in Moscow on 24 April 1997 setting ceilings on the number of ground forces, tactical air forces and anti-aircraft personnel that could be deployed in the 100km zone on each side of China's border with the former Soviet republics. The agreement does not, however, cover the strategic components of the armed forces, strategic missile forces or long-range aviation. The ceiling figures will not be made public until the agreement has been ratified by the parliaments of all five countries, although Russian defence sources state that the figures include 130,400 ground forces and 3,900 tanks for China, and the same again for Russia, Kazakstan, Kyrgyzstan and Tajikistan combined. Yet the agreement will not actually reduce the number of forces on either side, since the current number of forces deployed by all five countries is already well below the ceiling levels.[4]

During Yeltsin's second visit to China, he and President Zemin also confirmed that they would continue their negotiations on the remaining border issues. In May 1991, Russia and China had signed an Agreement on the Eastern Section of the Boundary followed by an Agreement on the Western Section of the Boundary in September 1994. Yet two islands near Khabarovsk and one in the Argun River remain disputed. These border Agreements are constantly under attack from the nationalist opposition in Russia, and from regional leaders in the Russian Far East. However, except for the islands still in dispute, the demarcation of the Sino-Russian border has been almost finalised according to the two boundary agreements, and Foreign Minister Primakov declared in January 1997 that the demarcation would be complete by the end of the year.[5]

While confirming the promotion of military exchanges and increased cooperation on military technology, Presidents Yeltsin and Jiang stressed that developing such military ties was not directed against any third country or group of countries. Although they announced no new Russian arms sale to China, agreement had been reached on the licensed production and purchase of additional Su-27 aircraft during Vice-Chairman of China's Central Military Commission Liu Huaqing's visit to Russia in December 1995. China currently has 33 Su-27 and four Su-27B, and is to produce up to 150 Su-27 under licence from Russia.[6] It has also been reported that China is seeking to purchase destroyers and other naval vessels from Moscow, as well as armoured personnel carriers.[7]

During Yeltsin's 1996 visit to China, the two sides signed an agreement to cooperate on the joint development of energy resources. Both China and Russia see the energy sector as a priority area for bilateral cooperation. Trade relations, however, have not been strengthened as Russia had expected and fluctuated from $4.4bn in 1992 to $4.2bn in 1995, despite a sharp increase in 1993 to $5.4bn. In 1995, Russia accounted for only 2% of China's total trade, while Japan, the US and South Korea accounted for 20%, 13.8% and 6% respectively. In turn, China was responsible for only 3.4% of Russia's total trade, while Germany and the US accounted for 10.2% and 6.3% respectively.[8] As a result, Yeltsin stated that the two countries should aim for a $20bn bilateral trade turnover by 2000. Border trade is an important component, but it has been restricted by issues of quality control and currency inconvertibility.

By the end of 1993, the government in Moscow and the authorities in the Far Eastern region were becoming deeply concerned about the scale of illegal Chinese immigration into the region.[9] As a result, the Russian government tightened its entry requirements and customs procedures, causing the total trade turnover in 1994 to drop to $3.8bn from the 1993 figure of $5.4bn. Against this background, Russia and China stressed in their 1996 Joint Statement that they were ready to continue their efforts towards 'a healthy and orderly development of exchanges' between their border areas, implying that Moscow and Beijing share concerns about the illegal and large-scale immigration of Chinese over the border into the Russian Far East.

The Joint Statement made no direct reference to the situation on the Korean Peninsula. According to the official press briefing held after the summit, Moscow proposed holding an international conference attended by all the countries concerned – North and

South Korea, China, the US, Russia and Japan. China responded simply by stating that North–South talks were important, demonstrating its cautious attitude to Russia's involvement on the Peninsula.

On the issue of security and cooperation in the Asia-Pacific region more generally, both powers attached importance to regional security dialogue and cooperation. China does not support a collective regional security system, preferring bilateral arrangements instead. Russia maintains that a multilateral regional security system is a long-term objective, but, in contrast to the previous Soviet approach, has ceased to propose unrealistic multilateral security projects. Accordingly, both sides have a similar approach to regional security, reflected in the Joint Statement which stressed the importance of bilateral and regional security dialogues, as well as the need to strengthen regional security cooperation by reaching consensus step-by-step through consultations.

Trends

In contrast to his first two state visits to China in 1992 and 1994, Yeltsin's 1996 visit added a rhetorical aspect to Sino-Russian relations. But, despite the hyperbole of the 'strategic partnership', the two powers have on the whole been guided by practical security and economic interests and the wish to normalise their bilateral relations. Stable relations between Russia and China would contribute to the stability of the whole Asia-Pacific region, which is clearly in the interests of the West. Although the US factor has played a role in the rhetoric of Sino-Russian relations, from a political, economic and security perspective, both Russia and China continue to place top priority on their relationship with the US. Both countries are also attempting to maintain and develop relations with the major Asia-Pacific powers, such as Japan and India, which helps to increase their diplomatic manoeuvrability. Moreover, apart from the sense that each poses a threat against the other, stronger on the Russian side, the two countries have no common vital security interests or values – such as ideology, freedom or democracy –

Russia and China have no common vital security interests

through which to establish or sustain allied relations. It is therefore unrealistic to believe that China and Russia will form an anti-US or anti-Western military alliance in the foreseeable future.

This does not, however, exclude the possibility that both powers might, from time to time, for domestic and external political reasons, choose to present a unified position, particularly against the US, to demonstrate their rejection of pressure from Washington or against what they see as the 'US-dominated unipolar system' in the international arena. During Chinese Prime Minister Li Peng's visit to Moscow on 26–28 December 1996, Yeltsin stated that there should not be leading and led countries in the world, and that a strategic Sino-Russian partnership would contribute to a multipolar international order. Li Peng responded that China also opposed a unipolar world, and that multipolarisation could only benefit the world order.[10] The 'multipolar international order' has become a cliché both of Russian diplomacy and of Sino-Russian relations. This common position was reaffirmed by the Joint Statement on Global Multipolarisation and the Establishment of a New World Order signed by Yeltsin and Jiang in Moscow on 23 April 1997, in which both countries agreed to promote global multipolarisation.[11] They also expressed concern about international attempts to enlarge and strengthen military blocs – by which Russia implicitly meant NATO enlargement, and China meant US–Japanese security relations. In this context it is interesting to note that then Defence Minister Rodionov, during his visit to Japan in May 1997, gave a positive assessment of the development of the Japan–US security relationship, including a review of the 1978 Guidelines for Japan–US Defence Cooperation, at which China repeatedly expressed its concern. This clearly demonstrates that Russia and China have different attitudes towards Japan–US security relations.[12]

To present a unified position is one thing, but whether such a position can bring about any real political change is quite another. So far at least, a unified Sino-Russian position has created no tangible political result. Indeed, Russia and China have had difficulty agreeing on many specific issues. As was demonstrated during Yeltsin's visit to Beijing in 1996, China is happy to support Russia when the issue concerned does not affect its own interests or influence, for example, NATO enlargement. China's opposition to

NATO enlargement in fact had no impact on the process. However, while Russia might expect to play a greater role in the Asia-Pacific region, China will not support Russia where its critical interests are at stake or where its own influence might be challenged. This was clearly demonstrated by China's cautious attitude to Russia's involvement in the Korean Peninsula issue. There is thus a limit to the viability and unity of the positions the two countries can adopt, even on a case-by-case basis.

Whether Russian policy towards China will continue on its current course in the long term is unclear because of the uncertainty and unpredictability surrounding the future of the two countries. Russia's relationship with China could sour if, with its strengthened military power, China becomes more assertive in the Asia-Pacific region, or indeed if Russia does so. China has a superior position to Russia in the region both politically and economically, and Russia must accept a junior partnership with China – a potential source of frustration for Moscow, especially given the nationalistic domestic atmosphere.

Russia must accept a junior partnership with China

Many Russians, anxiously surveying their vast and empty Far Eastern territories, their sluggish economy and the large number of Chinese immigrants in the region, believe that sharing borders with an economically booming China which may become an assertive superpower makes Russia vulnerable. This sense of insecurity has even been voiced by high-ranking officials. In a speech in Moscow on 26 December 1996, then Defence Minister Rodionov cited China as one of the few countries that could pose a military threat to Russia. Although the Russian Foreign Ministry immediately brushed aside this comment as unauthorised, few in Moscow doubted that Rodionov's statement reflected suspicions harboured at the highest levels of the national-security structure.[13] These views held by the political élite could alter the direction of Russia's China policy, or at least create a discrepancy between its rhetoric and its actual implementation. It should also be noted that 'Eurasianism', one of the current trends in promoting relations with China, is closely connected with Russian conservatism and nationalism which could also create a negative climate for the relationship with China.

Another potential area of tension is Central Asia. A major tenet of Moscow's foreign policy is to extend its protection to the ten million or so Russians resident in Central Asia, and preserve stability along the region's vital southern borders, which Russia continues to see as its own defensible borders. China, for its part, is counting on the Central Asian states becoming market economies. Increased economic and trade links between Central Asia and China could raise China's political influence in the region at Russia's expense, which could become a potential cause of tension in the future. China has separatist problems in its Xinjiang province and is concerned that the ethnic influence from Central Asia may spill over the border into areas with large Uighur, Kazak and Kyrgyz populations.

Russian arms sales and transfers of military technology to China also have potential strategic implications. There are concerns among China's neighbours that the strategic balance in North-east Asia is shifting. Given that China is placing top priority on economic growth and is suffering from budget deficits, its defence modernisation is expected to proceed at a moderate rate. While imports of Russian arms and military technology are unlikely to alter the strategic balance in the near future, by continuing to supply advanced weaponry and technology to China – thus facilitating its military modernisation – Russia could eventually affect the long-term military balance in Asia. Moscow's justifies its military cooperation with China by claiming that Russia strictly observes international norms and is concerned to maintain the balance of power in the region, without jeopardising its own security. Nevertheless, because of the general lack of Russian policy coordination and the fragmented and sometimes contradictory directives, as well as insufficient transparency on details of the arms and military technology sold to China, it is not clear whether Moscow's reasoning is accurate. Doubt about Russia's real motives is one of the major reasons for regional concern about these sales, which will require careful and continued monitoring.

Given their current common interests and needs, Russia and China will continue to strengthen their cooperative relations, at least in the short term. But the relationship contains inherent tensions which could become overt in the long run if domestic and external circumstances change. Russia and China may at times adopt unified political positions, but there are limits to how unified such positions can be and whether they can have any serious political impact on Western interests.

chapter 3

Japan

In contrast to Sino-Russian relations, Russo-Japanese relations have undergone no significant improvement since the collapse of the Soviet Union. The relationship, however, has been gradually evolving and adjusting to the changing regional and international environment. The territorial dispute between Moscow and Tokyo over the four islands between the Sea of Okhotsk and the North Pacific remains a persistent source of tension between the two countries. In addition, Russia's domestic problems have caused some inconsistency in its policy objectives and their implementation, or a gap between rhetoric and real policy.

Soviet–Japanese relations were moulded by the Cold War. But even after its end and the major shift in policy of Gorbachev's 'new thinking', remnants of 'old thinking' persisted in Moscow's policy towards the Asia-Pacific region. This was particularly true of Soviet policy towards Japan, where its traditional stance on the territorial dispute remained substantially unchanged. For Russia, this issue has been the most difficult and complicated of all the Soviet legacies for its relations with the West and the Asia-Pacific region in particular. The dispute still yokes the Russo-Japanese relationship to the Second World War, and has until now prevented both countries from fully normalising bilateral relations and concluding a peace treaty.

The legacy of the past in both countries also has specific emotional and perceptive aspects. The Japanese remain distrustful of Russia as a result of past traumas.[1] Russians too, partly as a result of Soviet education, are suspicious of Japan because of their past relationship and the territorial issue.[2] These persistent negative attitudes are difficult to overcome and place specific constraints on the bilateral relationship.

To Russia, Japan has four main characteristics. First, it is a major Western power with one of the strongest economies. Second, it is a primary Asia-Pacific power, a region to which Russia attaches increasing importance. Third, it is an ally of the US, which maintains a military presence on its territory. Fourth, Japan is not only a key economic power, but is also becoming a major political actor. Russia, therefore, has political, economic and security reasons for improving its relations with Japan. These include:

- using Japan's economic resources to further its own economic reform, particularly in developing its Far Eastern region;
- ensuring the geostrategic stability of its eastern border;
- gaining Japanese support for Russia's participation in international economic systems, such as the World Trade Organisation and the Paris Club, as well as in the political and economic processes of the Asia-Pacific.

President Yeltsin and Foreign Minister Kozyrev even went so far as to suggest alignment with Japan. In February 1992, Yeltsin wrote a letter to then Japanese Prime Minister Kiichi Miyazawa in which he referred to Japan as 'a potential alliance partner'.[3] At the time, Yeltsin's wish to resolve the territorial issue promptly clearly corresponded with this rhetoric. Just before the collapse of the Soviet Union and less than a month after the victory of 'democratic forces' in the Moscow coup attempt of August 1991, Kozyrev had stated publicly:

> *Is it not time for us to settle the legacies of the past, for example, by expatriating Honecker to Germany, by returning islands we promised back in 1956 to Japan, and by re-establishing our Embassy in Israel?*[4]

Yeltsin himself maintained in May 1992 that he intended to sign a peace treaty with Japan during 1993.[5] The President's state visit to Japan in October 1993 created an important new foundation for the bilateral relationship as well as for negotiations on the territorial issue. But Russia's domestic political situation, including the rise in conservatism and nationalism and the foreign-policy shift away from its initial Western orientation, changed the environment of the bilateral relationship. Russia's domestic politics have become a powerful factor constraining Moscow's ability to settle the territorial issue. Both its 1992 rhetoric about 'alliance' and the desire to see the territorial issue resolved promptly have disappeared. In 1994, Foreign Minister Kozyrev explained that developing practical relations with Japan would raise the bilateral relationship to the level of a real partnership. As a result, it would become easier to resolve even the most difficult problems.[6]

Since the collapse of the Soviet Union, the relations among the major regional powers – the US, Japan, China and Russia – and the region's strategic environment have changed significantly. The success of Russia's attempts to democratise, create a market economy and practise diplomacy based on law and justice has become of vital interest to Japan. Japan's desire to play a greater role in the international arena requires it to cooperate more closely with Russia. Furthermore, the political and economic significance to the region of the autonomous Russian Far East has increased.

While the military threat Russia posed to Japan has reduced, other problems and potential threats have taken its place. These have their origin in the socioeconomics of the Russian Far East, and include environmental problems and rising crime, all of which require Japan to cooperate with the Russian government and the Russian Far Eastern authorities.

Japan's long-standing approach to the territorial dispute, in response to the hardline Soviet position, had been to adopt the 'principle of inseparability of political and economic relations'.[7] This meant that without progress on the territorial

from 'inseparability of political and economic relations' to 'expanded equilibrium'

issue there could be no progress in other areas. Tokyo thus explicitly linked economic and other relations to the disputed islands.

But during the Gorbachev and early Yeltsin years, Japan adjusted to the new international environment by gradually changing its basic approach from exclusively economic and political ties with Russia to a more positive, expanded equilibrium between the two countries. This so-called 'principle of expanded equilibrium' is intended to develop the overall Russo-Japanese relationship by balancing progress in political relations – at whose core lies resolving the territorial issue – and economic relations.[8]

A New Foundation for the Relationship

Yeltsin's state visit to Japan from 11–13 October 1993 created a new foundation for Russo-Japanese relations. At the end of the visit, Yeltsin and Prime Minister Morihiro Hosokawa signed both the Tokyo Declaration and the Economic Declaration. The Tokyo Declaration established a clear basis for negotiations on the territorial issue. The two sides agreed that both countries should continue negotiations towards an early conclusion of a peace treaty by resolving their dispute over the four islands on the basis of historical and legal facts, the agreements between the two countries, and the rules of law and justice. Yeltsin's consent to the 'early' conclusion of a peace treaty indicated his concern to resolve the issue promptly. The Russian President also demonstrated his willingness to withdraw his military forces from the islands, which Japan has consistently demanded since the Soviet Union began to build up its armed presence there in 1978. Already in May 1992, he had announced that all Russian military troops, except for border guards, would be withdrawn. In Tokyo in October 1993, he told Prime Minister Hosokawa that half the troops had been withdrawn and that the other half would definitely leave.

The two leaders also confirmed the importance of political dialogue, and agreed to broaden talks between their two governments on a wide range of issues, including security. They signed an agreement to eliminate nuclear weapons in Russia and to establish a joint committee to oversee this. Based on this agreement, the two sides agreed to bilateral projects including financial support from Japan to construct facilities in Russia to store nuclear material retrieved from dismantled warheads, as well as facilities to process liquid radioactive wastes in Vladivostok, and to treat liquid missile fuel.[9]

In their Economic Declaration, Japan and Russia agreed to develop trade and economic relations on the basis of the 'principle of expanded equilibrium'. Specific areas for cooperation included

energy, transport, telecommunications, converting military industries, the safety of nuclear-power plants and environmental
conservation.

The Territorial Dispute

When the Tokyo Declaration was signed in October 1993,
negotiations to resolve the territorial dispute were expected to start
promptly. In high-level talks following Yeltsin's visit to Japan, Russia
repeatedly confirmed that Russo-Japanese relations should be
advanced on the basis of the Declaration. However, with the
growing nationalism and conservatism of Russia's domestic politics,
Moscow became wary of dealing with the territorial issue and began
to avoid negotiations altogether. This demonstrated clear inconsistency between Russia's rhetoric on the issue and its real policy.

Against this background, Prime Minister Tomiichi Murayama
sent a message to President Yeltsin in September 1995 in which he
stressed that both countries should continue their negotiations based
on the Tokyo Declaration and resolve the territorial dispute. In reply,
Yeltsin stated that while Russia was committed to furthering its
cooperation with Japan in all areas in accordance with the Tokyo
Declaration, the difficult issues between the two countries should be
resolved calmly and without haste, taking into account the realities
of the situation and with due consideration to the interests of the
peoples of both countries. This message made clear that Yeltsin's
readiness to resolve the territorial issue promptly had evaporated
and that Russia was not yet ready to begin negotiations. In January
1996, just after assuming the post of Foreign Minister, Primakov
even suggested that resolving the territorial dispute should be left to
the next generation.

In April 1996, Prime Minister Ryutaro Hashimoto was in
Moscow to attend the Group of Seven (G-7) two-day nuclear
summit. Given the fluidity of Russia's domestic politics, both sides
clearly wanted to prevent the territorial issue becoming a political
pawn in the forthcoming June presidential election campaign. On 19
April, during their bilateral meeting, Yeltsin and Hashimoto agreed
to revitalise the peace treaty negotiations at Foreign Minister level
after the Russian elections. Yeltsin also reiterated that both Russia
and Japan should pursue the peace treaty based on realism through

broad bilateral exchanges and good relations.[10] This agreement has not, however, been reflected in Russia's actual policy.

When Foreign Minister Primakov visited Japan from 14–17 November 1996, he was reluctant to negotiate the substance of the territorial issue, although he did not repeat his claim that resolving the dispute would be left to the next generation. Japanese Foreign Minister Yukihiko Ikeda stressed the importance of advancing negotiations on the territorial issue and creating an appropriate environment in which to resolve it, and that both should proceed in parallel. Primakov stated that an appropriate environment for resolving the dispute should be created first, but he did not commit himself to starting negotiations towards resolving the territorial issue. He also proposed 'joint economic activities' on the four disputed islands.[11] Referring to the Falkland Islands, he suggested marine-product processing, travel infrastructure and transport as areas for joint economic activity. Primakov recommended that both sides discuss principles and frameworks for these activities, and stressed the need for both sides to maintain their own positions on sovereign rights to the disputed islands. Ikeda argued that Russia's proposal of joint economic activities should not ignore or be a substitute for the issue of sovereign rights to the disputed islands, but also stated that if Russia were to present a concrete proposal for such activities, Japan would study it.[12]

President Yeltsin also touched on the idea of joint economic activities in his annual address to the Russian parliament on 6 March 1997.[13] In this address he stated that Moscow would attempt to reinvigorate its dialogue with Japan, and, confirming its allegiance to the Tokyo Declaration, expressed his government's readiness to develop relations with Japan in all areas, including the proposed joint economic development of 'the South Kuril islands'.[14] This may be an indication at the highest level that Moscow is ready to negotiate 'joint economic activities' on the four disputed islands, but not to negotiate on their sovereignty.

As for the demilitarisation of the disputed islands, during Foreign Minister Ikeda's visit to Moscow in March 1996, Foreign Minister Primakov explained that Russia was attempting to demilitarise the islands, and that the number of Russian military troops currently stationed there was around 3,500, with none on

Shikotan island.[15] This was the first official communication on the state of the military withdrawal since Yeltsin's announcement in Tokyo in October 1993 that all Russian troops would leave the islands. During his visit to Japan in November 1996, Primakov reaffirmed the total withdrawal of Russian military troops from the island. This process of withdrawal, however, should be seen as part of the overall reduction in the military forces deployed in the Russian Far East, and not as a sign that Russia is softening its position on the territorial dispute itself.

Russia and Japan attach importance to creating an appropriate environment for resolving the issue. Both governments are encouraging mutual visits by the Russian inhabitants of the four islands and Japanese citizens without a passport or visa, in accordance with the framework established in 1991. Since then, more than 3,600 people from both Russia and Japan have taken advantage of this exchange programme, increasing mutual understanding between the Russian islanders and the Japanese. During Foreign Minister Primakov's visit to Tokyo in November 1996, both sides agreed to expand the framework of this exchange.

Japanese fishing in the territorial waters around the disputed islands has become a serious issue that needs to be addressed. In 1993, Russian border guards began shooting at Japanese fishermen found in 'the territorial waters' of the four islands. These incidents understandably increased political tension between the two countries. When Russia's then First Deputy Prime Minister Oleg Soskovets visited Japan in November 1994, he and then Japanese Foreign Minister Yohei Kono agreed on the need to ensure a stable fishing order in the islands' territorial waters and to begin negotiations on a mutually acceptable framework. Several inconclusive rounds of negotiations have been held since March 1995. During Primakov's visit to Japan in November 1996, he and Foreign Minister Ikeda agreed to continue efforts to reach an agreement.

Economic and Trade Relations
The turnover in Russo–Japanese trade dropped sharply from $5.4bn in 1991 to $3.5bn in 1992, before gradually increasing to $6.0bn in 1995, close to the peak of Soviet–Japanese trade in 1989 of $6.1bn.[16]

However, Russia accounted for only 0.8% of Japan's total trade in 1995, while Japan accounted for only 3.2% of Russia's total trade the same year.[17] The stagnation of Japanese exports at a low level has marked Russian–Japanese trade since 1992. While in 1995 Russian imports stood at $4.8bn, a 34% increase from the previous year, Japanese exports remained at $1.2bn, the same level as the previous year and only an 8% increase from 1992.[18] The total amount of foreign direct investment in 1995 was $2.8bn – of which $75m came from Japan, $810m from the US, $420m from Germany and $110m from the UK.[19]

Japanese companies are still cautious about exporting to or investing in Russia without government-backed finance or trade insurance, such as the Export–Import Bank loan and government export insurance. This caution stems from Russia's record of not settling its past commercial debts – in 1996 it still owed $1.1bn to Japanese trading companies – its inadequate legal and taxation systems, and the other economic problems in the Russian Far East examined in Chapter 1, which all seriously reduce the export and investment incentives of Japanese enterprises. Although Tokyo is committed to extending both the Export–Import Bank loan and its export insurance to a total of $4.1bn as part of its aid for Russia's economic reforms, Russia has still not used a large part of these funds, for domestic reasons.

Russia is pursuing several projects for economic cooperation in the Russian Far East with the Japanese and US private sectors. The most promising are the Sakhalin-1 and Sakhalin-2 projects to develop oil and gas off Sakhalin island. Russia signed contracts for both projects with Japanese and US enterprises to a total value of nearly $20bn, which entered into force in June 1996 after the Duma passed a law on production-sharing in December 1995. Russia expects the future success of these projects to encourage further foreign investment in its Far East. But how these schemes will actually develop, given Russia's various internal problems remains to be seen.

During his visit to Japan in November 1994, First Deputy Prime Minister Soskovets and Foreign Minister Kono agreed to establish the Russian–Japanese Inter-Governmental Commission on Trade and Economy. During the Soviet era, establishing such a Commission had long been requested by Moscow, and since the collapse of the Union, Japan and Russia's consultative forum on economic matters had only been at vice-ministerial level. The Commission is headed by Russia's First Deputy Prime Minister and by the Japanese Foreign Minister, who supervise and coordinate the ministries responsible for economic and trade matters in the expectation that issues will be solved by prompt decision-making at the political level. Three sub-commissions were also created in July 1995: the first was established to improve conditions for bilateral trade and economic relations; the second was established to facilitate the use of assistance for Russia's market economic reforms; and the third was established to handle Japan's economic relations with the Russian Far East.

Russia's primary motive in setting up the Commission was to create a high-level institution through which to channel more Japanese finances into the Russian economy, in particular to the Russian Far East. Japan, for its part, expects to use this forum to overcome obstacles to economic and trade relations created by Russia's outstanding debt and other domestic problems, and to strengthen trade and economic relations with the Russian Far East, but not to commit itself to providing new financial resources. Despite these different expectations, establishing the Commission has broadened the structure of Russian–Japanese relations, in particular by increasing bilateral political dialogue on economic and trade issues, which had not existed during the Soviet era.

Security Relations
Since the dissolution of the Soviet Union, the Russo-Japanese security dialogue has steadily developed. It now includes bilateral policy-planning talks; exchanges of defence scholars; annual consultations on preventing incidents at sea beyond the territorial waters and the air-space above them; and the Japanese, Russian and US Trilateral Forum on North Pacific Security. As mentioned above, Russia and Japan have also begun to cooperate on eliminating nuclear weapons and nuclear waste.

During his visit to Moscow in March 1996, Japanese Foreign Minister Ikeda and Russian Foreign Minister Primakov agreed that Japan's Defence Agency and Russia's Defence Ministry should begin ministerial-level exchanges.[20] A new pillar of dialogue – security dialogue – was thus established to complement the political and economic pillars. Following this agreement, Japan's then Minister of State and Director-General of the Defence Agency Hideo Usui visited Russia in April 1996. This was the first time in the history of the countries' bilateral relations, including during the Soviet and tsarist periods, that a Japanese Defence Minister had visited Russia. At a meeting with Russia's then Defence Minister Pavel Grachev, both sides confirmed their commitment to continued and strengthened dialogue and exchanges on security issues. They signed a document agreeing to implement various confidence-building measures, including enhancing transparency, mutual notification of large-scale exercises and exchange visits by naval vessels.[21] Former Russian Defence Minister Igor Rodionov, in turn, visited Japan in May 1997 and agreed with his counterpart on measures to strengthen the Russian–Japanese security dialogue and further exchanges, including establishing a working group to study confidence-building measures.[22]

Trends

Russia and Japan have been steadily broadening their relationship since the collapse of the Soviet Union, reflecting their common interests, although it has not yet been sufficiently consolidated. Nevertheless, the territorial dispute and inadequate high-level political dialogue distinguish Russian–Japanese relations from Russia's relationship with the other major Western powers or with China. It is symbolic that after Yeltsin's visit to Japan in October 1993, no summit meeting was held between the two countries until that between Prime Minister Hashimoto and President Yeltsin in April 1996. However, political dialogue between the two countries broadened in 1996 to encompass security and the economy. But, with the basis of the relationship still not solid, the current upbeat process cannot last without continued government efforts to sustain political momentum.

the basis of the relationship is still not solid

The territorial issue will remain a major cause of tension between Russia and Japan. Although both sides have repeatedly confirmed their commitment to the Tokyo Declaration, they have different approaches to resolving the territorial issue. Japan is keen to negotiate a quick solution, while Russia now wants to avoid negotiations for domestic political reasons. In focusing on developing security and economic cooperation with Japan, Moscow is attempting to minimise the damaging effect the dispute would otherwise have on bilateral relations. The discrepancy between Russia's rhetoric confirming the Tokyo Declaration and its actual policy has frustrated Japan and limits the degree to which the relationship can develop further. At the same time, Russia and Japan want to avoid any tensions created by the territorial issue. Both sides are thus actively engaged in negotiations on fishing in the territorial waters of the four islands as a transitional measure until the dispute is finally resolved. The success of these negotiations will not only reduce the frequency and magnitude of tensions caused by Japanese fishing in these waters, but will also enhance other potential cooperative projects related to the four islands.

Although economic interests underlie most of Russia's policy towards Japan, bilateral trade and economic relations have not progressed as Russia had expected. Russia's domestic economic problems have imposed severe constraints on its plans to use Japan's economic power to further economic reform and development in the Russian Far East. The main achievement in this area was the establishment of the bilateral Inter-Governmental Commission to consult on economic and trade issues at the political level, thus helping to create a more favourable environment for private-sector industry. But the substance of Russia's future economic ties with Japan undoubtedly depends on the progress of its domestic economic reforms.

As a result of the changed strategic structure of North-east Asia, both countries have a common interest in developing their security ties. Needless to say, there are also limitations here. Russia cannot, for example, expect to engage in arms sales or military cooperation that might damage the Japanese–US security alliance. Russo-Japanese security relations will thus remain primarily in the areas of security dialogue, exchanges and confidence-building measures. Since Russia appears to accept the need to tone down its ambitions in this area, its stated security-policy objectives and their implementation are likely to remain compatible, at least in the short term.

Both governments will maintain their efforts to broaden bilateral ties and build up a stable relationship. However, the territorial dispute and Russia's political and economic situation impose clear constraints on the dynamics of the bilateral relationship.

chapter 4

The Korean Peninsula

In most respects, Russia's policy towards the Korean Peninsula has mirrored its foreign policy towards China and Japan. This chapter examines Russian engagement on the Peninsula and its bilateral relations with South and North Korea.

The early Yeltsin administration, attracted by South Korean economic power, initially attempted to develop close relations with Seoul based on the diplomatic relationship established by Gorbachev in September 1990. Economically, Russia expected to use South Korea's growing economic power to develop its Far East. Politically, the Korean Peninsula is an area of strategic importance where the interests of major powers – namely the US, China, Japan and Russia – intersect, and where the US maintains a military presence. Russia strongly wishes to become involved with the Korean Peninsula, an area that affects its security and its political presence in North-east Asia.

South Korea, for its part, enhanced its international position and increased its political advantage over North Korea when it established diplomatic relations with the Soviet Union and subsequently developed relations with Russia. Seoul also expects Russia to continue to suspend its military assistance to North Korea which would allow the South to maintain its strategic advantage over its neighbour. At the same time the South has been cautious about Russia's involvement on the Peninsula.

By normalising and developing its relations with South Korea, Moscow dampened its relations with the North. The collapse of the eastern bloc's communist regimes and the loss of Soviet and later Russian support intensified North Korea's economic crisis and weakened its military strength. This reduced Russia's influence over North Korea, which had anyway been minimal. Even during the Soviet era, North Korea could not be considered part of the Soviet sphere of influence. Until Sino-Soviet relations began to improve, North Korea played both powers off against each other to maximise the support it received from both.[1] Gorbachev wrote in his memoirs that as a result of Sino-Soviet conflict, Moscow and Beijing competed for influence over Pyongyang which actually received greater support from both sides as a reward for its relative neutrality.[2]

However, Yeltsin's initial South Korean-oriented policy did not satisfy Russia's hopes of large-scale South Korean capital to develop its Far Eastern region. Worst of all, Russia was marginalised during the most significant North-east Asian diplomatic and strategic confrontation of the early post-Cold War era – that over North Korea's nuclear status. Russia's élite perceived this as a loss of the prestige the country had enjoyed in North-east Asia during the Soviet era, provoking considerable opposition to Moscow's Korea policy. Opposition pressure, combined with Moscow's own frustration at its inability to influence events on the Peninsula, led the Yeltsin government to modify its South Korean-oriented regional policy and to attempt to improve its relations with the North.

Russia's Disengagement from the Korean Peninsula

North Korea was faced with almost total international isolation and severe economic disruption after the Soviet Union – later Russia – and China normalised relations with South Korea. To secure the survival of the state and its regime, Pyongyang played the nuclear card. On 12 March 1993, it announced its intended withdrawal from the Nuclear Non-Proliferation Treaty (NPT). This action, together with the death of Kim Il Sung on 8 July 1994, heightened the uncertainty and tension on the Korean Peninsula. The outcome of the nuclear issue will affect not only the viability of the NPT regime as a whole, but also peace and stability on the Peninsula and in East Asia in general.

A nuclear-free Korean Peninsula would increase Russia's security, and Moscow has thus consistently supported the North–South Joint Declaration on the Denuclearisation of the Korean Peninsula signed on 31 December 1991. To Russia, it was therefore natural that, as a major power, it should be involved in negotiations on the North Korean nuclear issue. However, once bilateral negotiations began between Washington and Pyongyang, Russia was completely left out of the process. The US initially encouraged other nations to impose multilateral economic sanctions against North Korea. When this attempt failed, the US decided to negotiate directly with North Korea. The result of these negotiations was an Agreed Framework document, signed by the US and North Korea on 21 October 1994.[3]

Russia resents being left out of Korean talks

In this document, North Korea agreed to freeze its graphite-moderated reactors and related facilities, eventually dismantle them, allow the International Atomic Energy Agency (IAEA) to monitor this freeze, and remain a party to the NPT. In return, the US agreed to organise an international consortium to finance and supply light-water reactors and heavy oil to North Korea as an interim source of energy. The Agreement on the Establishment of the Korean Peninsula Energy Development Organisation (KEDO) was signed by the US, South Korea and Japan in March 1995. The fact that the diplomatic efforts to solve the crisis caused by North Korea's withdrawal from the NPT were primarily led by the US increased Moscow's resentment and intensified domestic opposition to its Korean policy. Foreign Minister Kozyrev complained that the US was ignoring Russia in its efforts to resolve the issue.[4] Moscow's proposals for a multilateral eight-party conference – including North and South Korea, the US, China, Russia, Japan, the UN and the IAEA – was not supported by the countries concerned, few of which had any interest in Russia's involvement on the Peninsula.

Russia was also angered by the fact that, in accordance with the March 1995 agreement, KEDO was to provide South Korean standard light-water nuclear reactors to the North. Besides its political interest in the issue, Russia, strongly lobbied by its nuclear-energy sector, had economic reasons for wishing to supply its own light-water reactors. Since the Soviet Union had dominated North Korea's nuclear industry market, and the two countries had signed an agreement for Russia to build a nuclear-power plant in North Korea in 1985, Moscow saw the provision of South Korean standard light-water reactors to North Korea as the loss of a market as well.

While trying to weaken the Armistice Agreement – signed in June 1953 by the two Koreas, the US and China – by withdrawing its personnel from the Military Armistice Commission, North Korea began to propose direct negotiations with the US to establish a new peace and security system. Pyongyang issued statements in March and April 1996 claiming that it had become impossible to maintain the status of the demilitarised zone between the North and the South. As a result, North Korean troops armed with trench mortars entered the Panmunjom common guard area in April 1996. In response, US President Bill Clinton and South Korean President Kim Young Sam jointly proposed on 16 April 1996 that South Korea, North Korea, the US and China hold four-party talks aimed at establishing a lasting peace on the Peninsula, while confirming that a new framework for a permanent peace should be pursued bilaterally by the two Koreas. As the Soviet Union was not a signatory to the Armistice Agreement, there is a good reason why this proposal did not include Russia. Whatever the reason, however, Moscow has openly cast doubt on the proposal and, while supporting a renewed inter-Korean peace dialogue, has maintained that a comprehensive solution to the Peninsula's problems should be sought by an international conference attended by all parties concerned, including Russia.[5]

Managing the nuclear issue is only part of the larger problem of reconciling and reunifying the two Koreas. Given the uncertainty surrounding the viability of the North Korean polity and its economy, reunification, whether peaceful or not, is not a foregone conclusion. The security implications of reunification for neighbouring countries, including Russia, are serious and raise critical arms-control questions and speculation regarding the future of the US military presence there. Russia might therefore prefer a very gradual process of reunification – or even retaining the two separate Koreas – to the sudden change in the geopolitical and security environment that reunification would create. In any case, the potential security implications give Russia a strong interest in engaging with the problems of the Korean Peninsula.

The 1994 North Korean–US Agreed Framework and the 1996 South Korea–US proposal of four-party talks also had a significant impact on Russia's sense of its place in post-Cold War North-east Asia. Nostalgic for its former superpower status, Russia felt diplomatically and economically excluded from the Korean Peninsula. Criticism of the talks process, and of Moscow's South Korean-oriented policy, came from various political groups within Russia. As a result of

> *Russia felt diplomatically and economically excluded*

its disengagement from the Korean Peninsula, the Russian government has modified its South Korean-oriented foreign policy and increased its attempts to improve its bilateral relations with North Korea.

South Korea

Throughout most of 1992, the Yeltsin government placed coop-eration with South Korea well above relations with North Korea. In March 1992, Foreign Minister Kozyrev visited Seoul and assured Foreign Minister Lee Sang Ock that Russia would not cooperate with North Korea in developing its nuclear programme, and that Moscow had stopped selling offensive weapons to Pyongyang.[6]

In November 1992, Yeltsin paid a state visit to Seoul to formalise and strengthen links between the two countries. There he reiterated his support for peaceful reunification through North–South dialogue and repeated Kozyrev's claim that Russia had already stopped supplying offensive arms to the North. President Yeltsin and President Roh Tae Woo signed a treaty on the principles of their bilateral relations which proposed basing Russian–South Korean relations on the common ideals of freedom, democracy and commitment to a market economy. In an address to the South Korean National Assembly, Yeltsin expressed his government's intention to work as a partner with South Korea and Russia's desire to play a major role in establishing a new North-east Asian security system.[7] In a subsequent joint press conference, Yeltsin declared that the 1961 Soviet–North Korea Friendship and Mutual Assistance

Treaty would either be abolished or greatly revised. In particular, Moscow would consider repealing Article 1 of the Treaty which pledged the former Soviet Union to aid North Korea in the event of an attack by a third country. He also proposed multilateral consultations among the North-east Asian states as a preliminary step towards forming a consultative regional security body to mediate international disputes, and creating a centre for regional strategic research. On the Soviet–North Korea Friendship and Mutual Assistance Treaty, Yeltsin assured President Kim when he visited Moscow in June 1994 that amendments to the Treaty would no longer oblige Russia to side with North Korea in the event of a conflict.[8]

During Yeltsin's visit to Seoul in 1992, the two sides discussed major projects worth $20–30bn. Despite Russian hopes that improved relations with South Korea would help to transform the Russian economy, trade and economic links between the two countries remain modest. Although Russian trade with South Korea increased by 30% from $0.95bn in 1992 to $1.25bn in 1995, it accounted for only 1% of Russia's total trade turnover in 1995 (see Table 2, p. 22). Because of Russia's unfavourable investment environment, South Korean investment in its economy has been quite small. As of February 1995, South Korean firms had only invested $25m in the Russian economy as a whole. By January 1995, they had invested only $2.48m in Khabarovskii Krai, roughly 2% of the Far East's total foreign investment.[9] This disappointing reality reflected the similar problems faced by Russian–Japanese economic and trade relations.

Presidents Yeltsin and Roh Tae Woo also signed a memorandum providing for military exchanges and naval visits between Vladivostok and Pusan.[10] Later, in August 1993, then Deputy Prime Minister Aleksandr Shokhin visited Seoul and proposed that Russia would repay its debt to South Korea with weapons.[11] It was not until September 1994, however, that the two sides formally agreed that Moscow would repay part of its Korean debt with $187.5m-worth of weaponry which South Korea would use for military research.[12] Furthermore, the two sides agreed in July 1995 that Russia would repay $450m of its outstanding debt with raw materials, helicopters and further weapons.[13] However, the US disapproves of these transfers of Russian arms, and because the South Korean armed forces rely heavily on US weapon systems, the potential for further Russian arms sales to South Korea appears limited. In April 1997, just before his visit to South Korea, US Secretary of Defense William Cohen warned that it would be a political and military mistake for South Korea to accept Russia's offer of surface-to-air missiles, such as the SA-12, instead of buying US *Patriot* air-defence missiles, suggesting that the SA-12 might accidentally threaten US jets in any new Korean war. He also voiced concern about the 'inter-operability' of the SA-12 with the US F-15 and other military aircraft in South Korea.[14]

Russian arms sales to South Korea limited

When then Minister of Defence Grachev visited Seoul in May 1995, the two sides signed a memorandum on technological cooperation between their defence industries.[15] During a later visit to Seoul in December 1995, Prime Minister Viktor Chernomyrdin initialled the Declaration on the Development and Promotion of Trade, Economic, Science and Technology Cooperation, which lists military technology as one of the major fields of cooperation to be promoted.[16]

North Korea

As was the case with China, the early Western-oriented Yeltsin government had no reason to develop or even maintain relations with North Korea. Russia's economic problems did not even allow it to sustain the already cool relations it inherited following the establishment of diplomatic relations with South Korea in the final years of the Soviet Union. Moscow's policy had a devastating impact on North Korea. Russia virtually halted its military cooperation and arms exports to the North, and rejected the old Soviet trade policy based on barter and subsidies, demanding hard currency for its oil and food. Since barter trade with the Soviet Union comprised a large proportion of North Korea's total trade, Russia's new policy caused the North considerable hardship. Russian trade with North Korea declined by 70% from $292m in 1992 to $85m in 1995.

Even in the early days of the Yeltsin government, some in Russia were concerned at the country's loss of its already limited influence over North Korea. In July 1992, a Ministry of Foreign

Affairs statement stressed that Russia would not give in to pressure that aimed to put Russia in conflict with North Korea.[17] Domestic opposition to Russia's Korean policy came from a variety of sources. As with all foreign-policy issues, the communists were the most critical. However, questioning government policy was not limited to the hardliners. The general criticism was that Moscow, having renounced its ties with North Korea in an attempt to benefit from the economic potential of the South, had also given up its influence on the Korean Peninsula.[18]

Recognising that it had lost virtually all its authority on the Peninsula, Moscow began efforts to improve its relations with the North. During his visit to Pyongyang in January 1993, Deputy Foreign Minister Georgii Kunadze claimed that relations were recovering from their low point the previous year. He asserted that both sides needed each other economically, and stressed the need to preserve Russia's relations with North Korea to strengthen its role in the North-east Asian security structure.[19] The foreign-policy concept approved by Yeltsin in April 1993 also reiterated the need for Russia to maintain its influence over Pyongyang.[20] However, Russia's economic problems have severely limited these policy aspirations, since for North Korea the most important aspects of relations with Russia are economic and military assistance. Although there might be political mileage in subsidising the North Korean economy and military, Moscow clearly cannot afford to do so when it cannot even pay its own armed forces' wages. While both countries have an interest in improving bilateral relations, success has been limited by the fact that the great majority of Russian trade is based on market relations and conducted in convertible currency.

has Moscow lost its authority on the Peninsula?

On 7 August 1995, the Russian Foreign Ministry formally notified Pyongyang that Russia would renounce the 1961 Soviet–North Korea Friendship and Mutual Assistance Treaty when it expired on 10 September 1996, and proposed a draft of a new treaty. In September 1996, North Korea proposed a counter-draft, and negotiations on a new treaty were held in Pyongyang in January 1997. Clearly, a new treaty will be different from the previous alliance and will not include a military intervention clause. Instead, Russia may try to add some form of consultation clause to ensure a legal basis for its involvement, should a major crisis break out on the Korean Peninsula.

Trends

The Russian government now seems to be correcting its earlier South Korean-oriented policy to adopt more balanced relations with both Koreas. This will give it some influence with both, allowing it some say in the Peninsula's future. However, there are many constraints and few levers for Russia to implement such a policy. Relations with the two Koreas are interlinked and Russia cannot afford to jeopardise its relations with the South by giving economic and military assistance or political support to the North. Because of this dilemma, Russia will take a multilateral approach to its involvement on the Peninsula. But with no basic change in the situation on the Korean Peninsula, this approach has little prospect of support from the countries concerned, at least in the short run.

The fundamental reason for Russia's disengagement from the Korean Peninsula is not a lack of balanced relations with the two Koreas. The US, China and Japan, for example, have no such balanced relations. Should Moscow achieve such a balance, to what extent could it influence both Koreas to guarantee Russia an influential role on the Peninsula? The real reason for Russia's marginalisation is its weakened political, military and economic power. This same reason underlies Russia's current peripheral role in the Asia-Pacific as a whole. The US and South Korea have both been cautious about involving Russia in the talks on the future of the Peninsula. North Korea, for its part, sees no merit in including Russia, which Pyongyang fears may increase external pressure on it. Russia, in turn, may expect China to support its involvement on the Peninsula, but, as analysed in Chapter 2, China is not an active supporter. On the Korean Peninsula, a discrepancy between Russia's policy objectives and their implementation, and a distinction between real Russian influence and illusory Soviet influence – for which the Russian élite remains nostalgic – will therefore remain.

conclusion

Conclusion

Despite Moscow's frustration at its marginal role in much of North-east Asia, its regional diplomacy has been relatively restrained and less assertive than the high-handed, military-backed approach of the Soviet era. Moscow's current diplomacy also contrasts with its assertiveness towards the US, Europe and the CIS, exemplified in its attitude towards NATO enlargement and CIS integration. These contrasts reflect the different positions held by Russia's political élite and the degree of interest perceived as being at stake. Moscow's relations with the US and Western Europe have also influenced its approach to North-east Asia. Russia's foreign-policy shift away from its initial Western orientation has been mirrored in its relations with Japan, South Korea and China.

Russia's basic approach to its relations with these three countries has been relatively pragmatic and realistic, guided by practical security and economic interests and closely related to the security and economic environment of the Russian Far East. Recent developments in these relationships demonstrate that Russia has been making progress in building up bilateral relations, although to different degrees. At the same time, each bilateral relationship has its own inherent tensions. Russia's political and economic difficulties – including the economic crisis in its Far East – have prevented it from realising its policy objectives and has created a discrepancy between these objectives and their implementation.

While relations among the major regional powers have become more compatible since the end of the Cold War, Russia's current links with the region have been heavily weighted towards China, and its relations with China are heavily weighted towards security and arms sales. This structure in itself does not directly concern the West. However, its imbalance is not desirable for Russia, whose ultimate objectives are to ensure an influential role for itself in North-east Asia and the wider Asia-Pacific. Furthermore, this structure concerns Moscow because of the potential tensions underlying Sino-Russian relations and the feeling among Russians that China poses a threat. As examined in Chapter 2, this uneasiness has produced contradictory trends within the Russian government which could cause its China policy to fluctuate.

Russia's China policy could fluctuate

The unbalanced structure of Russia's regional relations is clearly related to the steady but slow improvement in its relations with Japan. The bilateral relationship with Japan thus has implications for Russia's overall geopolitical situation in the region. Russo-Japanese relationship, driven by the various factors examined in Chapter 3, has broadened its foundations to encompass both security and economics. These bases, however, are still not solid. The territorial issue remains a major obstacle and cause of tension. Russia has also failed to become involved in the critical negotiations surrounding the future of the Korean Peninsula. At the same time it is playing neither a negative nor a disruptive role in the process, despite its resentment at being excluded. Russia's disengagement from the Korean Peninsula has driven Moscow to review its South Korean-oriented foreign policy and attempt to develop more balanced relations with the two Koreas. But, as examined in Chapter 4, this has created a dilemma and leaves Russia few levers for achieving such balanced relations. So far, Moscow has made little progress in improving relations with Pyongyang.

In terms of its security, Russia has achieved significant and concrete arms-reduction and CBMs with China along their common borders. Russia has also improved its security relations with Japan and South Korea, particularly in the area of CBMs. This web of bilateral security ties could help to stabilise the security environment of North-east Asia. In terms of its economic and trade interests, however, Russia's achievements have not matched its aims and expectations. Bilateral trade has been sluggish, and trade turnover with the three major North-east Asian countries remains relatively low. Russia has had little success in securing external resources to help develop its Far Eastern region. The limits imposed by Russia's current economic problems also imply that its interdependence with the most important region of the Asia-Pacific remains weak. The only exception is Russia's arms sales to China. However, this in itself has a contradictory effect on Russian security and potentially negative strategic implications for regional security as a whole.

Reshaping Russian Policy

Various potential sources of political and security instability exist within the Asia-Pacific region, and North-east Asia in particular. The Korean Peninsula and Taiwan continue to be major focuses of regional security concerns. The high degree of unpredictability in the post-Cold War relationships of the four major powers – the US, Japan, China and Russia – and the balance of power among them complicate the region's politics and security.[1] The futures of Russia and China are also unpredictable and uncertain.

Since its emergence as an independent state, Russia has not been a major player in the Asia-Pacific, although its interests dictate that it must remain active and influential in the region. But more importantly, Russia has not been a negative or disruptive player either. However, the uncertainty surrounding Russia's domestic politics does not guarantee that it will continue to *relations with China are not a substitute for relations with the West* play this relatively neutral role. There is still a lack of consensus among the Asia-Pacific powers as to whether or how Russia should be engaged in the region's affairs.

Russia's place in the international arena undoubtedly depends on the future of its political and economic reforms. Russia needs to become a constructive player and to take some responsibility for maintaining regional peace and stability. This is in the interests of Russia, the region and the West as a whole. To this end, Russia must correctly understand its own interests, and above all that its relations with China are not a substitute for, or a counterbalance to, relations with the West.[2] No amount of wishful thinking can allow it to play the East off against the West. In this context, it is also extremely important for Russia to normalise its relations with Japan. This would improve its geopolitical position by correcting the current unbalanced structure of Russia's relations with North-east Asia. In this sense, the pending territorial issue with Japan will continue to impose constraints on Russia, not only in the bilateral, but also in the regional context.

To become a credible player in the Asia-Pacific region, Russia must strengthen the interdependence of its economy – and first of all that of its Far East – with those of North-east Asia. Most of the obstacles to strengthening its economic interdependence with, and integrating into, the region's economies stem from Russia's domestic problems. Russia's central and regional authorities must therefore implement a coherent policy and take concrete measures to improve the economic situation. If it is to attract private capital, it must create a favourable environment for investment, including better legal and administrative protection for commercial rights and a more rational tax system. Central government must allocate more financial resources based on the programme to develop the Far Eastern economy. However, as examined in Chapter 1, a gap between Moscow's rhetoric and real policy has already emerged. It may now be unrealistic to expect the government to provide even the projected financial resources for the development programme, since this would require a significant reallocation of budgetary resources which would not be politically feasible. The development programme states that local government and enterprises should share 50% of the total necessary funds. This means that central and local governments must implement appropriate policies to promote regional capital formation.

The Korean Peninsula is the main security issue in North-east Asia, and Russia resents the fact that its influence there has been marginalised by the other major powers. To counter this view, Moscow must demonstrate that it can and will play a constructive role on the Peninsula. The test will be whether Russia participates in, and how it contributes to, the KEDO process. Russia has a good knowledge of the nuclear-power-plant situation in North Korea as a result of Soviet–North Korean cooperation in this area. While KEDO will provide South Korean standard light-water reactors as specified in the US–North Korean Agreed Framework document, Russia could, for example, provide KEDO with technical assistance and information to facilitate the installation process.

Engaging Russia and Engagement in its Far East

An isolated, sullen, impoverished Russia would present a greater challenge to a stable world order than a healthy, competitive Russia that is part of that order.[3] Although Russia alone will decide its orientation, North-east Asian countries and the West could engage it further in the regional process and engage themselves further in the reform process in the Russian Far East.

Strong economic interdependence would give Russia not only rhetorical, but also substantial interests in the stability of the Asia-Pacific. Russia's central and regional governments must adopt appropriate policies and measures to develop its Far Eastern region and strengthen the country's interdependence with the Asia-Pacific economies. Engaging Russia in regional processes such as APEC is also necessary. Russia applied for membership of APEC in March 1995. New members will be elected in 1998 based on membership criteria to be decided in 1997, and these new members will participate in APEC from 1999. Membership alone will not strengthen the interdependence *admitting Russia to the APEC process* of Russia's economy with the Asia-Pacific or increase the influx of foreign capital into the country. But admitting Russia to APEC, if it meets the criteria, would encourage Moscow to take more measures to develop the Russian Far East and to share responsibility for the Asia-Pacific economic process by taking part in APEC's commitments, such as trade liberalisation.

The slow progress of political and economic reform in the Russian Far East and the region's nationalistic atmosphere created by its serious socioeconomic problems make Russia a less constructive partner in the Asia-Pacific. Yet on the other hand, the Russian Far East and Siberia are unquestionably major storehouses of energy and other resources required for the future growth of the dynamic Asian economies. Successful economic reform and development of the Russian Far East and Siberia would thus clearly be in the interests of the Asia-Pacific economies. It is in the interests of the Asia-Pacific, and more generally of the West, to support Russia's reforms and the development of its Far East. But it would be unrealistic to expect a major foreign-aid programme and there are clear limits to the degree of external cooperation or influence that can be brought to bear on Moscow. Various bilateral technical assistance programmes are already in place, and multilateral cooperation to reform the Russian Far East economy has also been pursued.

But there is room to increase cooperation among Japan, the US and major West European powers. A new process of cooperation between Asia and Europe began with the first summit of the Asia–Europe Meeting (ASEM) held in Bangkok in March 1996. The ASEM process is concerned not only with economic, but also political and security issues. Russia's foreign policy towards Western Europe and North-east Asia are interrelated: both regions share an interest in Russia's continuing political and economic reforms. North-east Asia, particularly Japan, the major West European powers and the US could thus pool their expertise and cooperate to help the reform process in the Russian Far East. Such cooperation could cover, for example, technical assistance for the administrative reform efforts of local governments, cooperation in tackling environmental problems, assistance in eliminating nuclear weapons and their platforms, and the re-education of military officers for new jobs.

Given the budgetary constraints facing the West, such coordinated assistance is becoming more necessary and would produce a more effective outcome than a less streamlined policy. Russia's neighbours to both the east and west share a desire to see Russia more integrated into both regions. But without domestic reform, Russia will be neither attractive as a partner nor capable of fulfilling its full potential. Russia's future in North-east Asia lies in its own hands.

notes

Notes

Chapter 1

[1] For the Soviet Union's relations with the Asia-Pacific region, see, for example, Gerald Segal, *The Soviet Union and the Pacific* (London: Unwin Hyman for the Royal Institute of International Affairs, 1990).
[2] Even the Soviet foreign-policy-makers and analysts publicly admitted that the Vladivostok initiative had produced poor results. See the discussion of Soviet foreign-policy-makers in 'The Vladivostok Initiative: Two Years On', *Mezhdunarodnaya Zhizn*, August 1988.
[3] For more details on Russia's foreign- and security-policy debate, see Renée de Nevers, *Russia's Strategic Renovation*, Adelphi Paper 289 (London: Brassey's for the IISS, 1994), pp. 23–39.
[4] *Ibid.*, p. 65.
[5] In his address to the National Assembly of the Republic of Korea made in November 1992, President Boris Yeltsin said: 'Nowadays our policy is being transferred from West European

and American lines to the Asia-Pacific region'. See *Rossiiskaya Gazeta*, 21 November 1992. On the eve of his January 1993 visit to India, Yeltsin stated: 'the recent series of state visits to South Korea, China and now to India is indicative of the fact that we are moving away from a Western emphasis'. See ITAR-TASS, 30 January 1993, cited in Radio Free Europe/Radio Liberty (RFE/RL) *Research Report*, vol. 2, no. 20, 14 May 1993, p. 52.
[6] Kyoji Komachi, 'Concept-Building in Russian Diplomacy: The Struggle for Identity from "Economization" to "Eurasiani-zation"', Paper No. 94-3, Center for International Affairs, Harvard University, Cambridge, MA, May 1994, pp. 27–28.
[7] *Ibid.*, p. 30.
[8] De Nevers, *Russia's Strategic Renovation*, p. 68.
[9] *Rossiiskaya Gazeta*, 25 February 1994, p. 7.
[10] Foreign Minister Yevgeni Primakov stressed this line at his first press conference after taking

office on 12 January 1996, and repeated it thereafter. See, for example, the interview with Primakov, 'Yevgeni Primakov Talks About Russia's Foreign Policy', *Rossiiskaya Gazeta*, 10 January 1997.

[11] Eastern Siberia is also relevant to an analysis of Russia's foreign policy towards Asia, particularly in terms of trade with the Asia-Pacific. However, this chapter deals mainly with the Russian Far East, since this region has direct security and economic implications for Russia's policy towards North-east Asia. On the Russian Far East, see John L. Stephan, *The Russian Far East: A History* (Stanford, CA: Stanford University Press, 1994).

[12] Mikhail Gorbachev wrote in his memoirs: 'the Soviet Union, based on the worst estimate of Chinese intention, took the basic course of building up its military forces in the Far East in the 1960s and 1970s'. See Gorbachev, *Gorbachev Kaisouroku*, vol. 2 (Tokyo: Shinchyousha, 1996), p. 500. *Kaisouroku* is the Japanese-language version of the memoirs, but the English-language edition does not contain this description.

[13] Interview with then Defence Minister Igor Rodionov, 'Russia's Defence Nearly Broken', *Trud*, 11 February 1997.

[14] *Defense of Japan* (Tokyo: Defense Agency of Japan, 1996), p. 41.

[15] Vladimir Portyakov, 'Migratsionnaya Situatsiya na Dalnem Vostoke Rossii', paper presented to the seminar 'Problems of Migration and Citizenship in the Post-Soviet Space', Moscow Center of the Carnegie Foundation, Moscow, 19 March 1995, pp. 16–17.

[16] Paul Dibb, *Towards a New Balance of Power in Asia*, Adelphi Paper 295 (Oxford: Oxford University Press for the IISS, 1995), pp. 90–91 and p. 93.

[17] Andrei Kozyrev, *Preobrazhenie* (Moscow: Mezhdunarodnoe otnoshenie, 1994), p. 244. Kozyrev stressed that the improved political climate in the Asia-Pacific and the improbability of large-scale military conflict in the region had radically changed Russia's approach to the security of its Asian regions, and that Russian military forces there would be reduced by 50% by 1995.

[18] Gerald Segal, 'Russia as an Asian-Pacific Power', in Ramesh Thakur and Carlyle A. Thayer (eds), *Reshaping Regional Relations: Asia-Pacific and the Former Soviet Union* (Boulder, CO: Westview Press, 1993), pp. 70–78.

[19] Kozyrev, *Preobrazhenie*, pp. 245–46.

[20] Vladimir Kolossov, 'The Russian Far East at the Crossroads: National and International Geopolitical Challenges', in Denis Roomley, Tatsuya Chiba, Akihiko Takagi and Yuriko Fukushima (eds), *Global Geopolitical Change and the Asia-Pacific: A Regional Perspective* (Aldershot: Avebury, 1996), p. 158.

[21] For a detailed analysis of the Russian Far East's regional development problems, see Sergei Manezhev, *The Russian Far East* (London: Royal Institute of International Affairs, 1993).

[22] Mark J. Valencia (ed.), *The Russian Far East in Transition: Opportunities for Regional Economic Cooperation* (Boulder, CO: Westview Press, 1995), p. 2.

[23] De Nevers, *Russia's Strategic Renovation*, pp. 14–15.

[24] Wakio Fujimoto, 'Roshia Kyokutou-chiiki no Seiji Jyoukyou: Enkaichihou wo chuushinni', in

Roshia-renpou Kyokutou-chiiki Kenkyuu (Tokyo: Japan Institute of International Affairs, 1996), p. 16.
[25] Interview with Governor of Khabarovskii Krai Viktor Ishaev, *Sevodnya*, 25 July 1996, p. 16.
[26] Kolossov, 'The Russian Far East at the Crossroads', p. 163.
[27] *Rossiiskie Vesti*, 9 January 1997.
[28] Interview with Governor Ishaev, *Sevodnya*, 25 July 1996.
[29] At a news conference in Moscow on 16 November 1996, Governor Ishaev stressed that illegal immigration by Chinese and North Koreans was the most serious threat to the Russian Far East. During the past five years, he stated, 500,000 out of a population of 8 million emigrated from the Russian Far East to central Russia, while illegal immigration by Chinese and North Koreans into the region has been increasing. *Moscow Broadcast*, 16 November 1996.
[30] Neil Malcolm, Alex Pravda, Roy Allison and Margot Light, *Internal Factors in Russian Foreign Policy* (Oxford: Oxford University Press for the Royal Institute of International Affairs, 1996), pp. 258–59.
[31] IISS, *The Military Balance 1996/97* (Oxford: Oxford University Press for the IISS, 1996), p. 275.
[32] *Ibid.*, p. 275.
[33] According to Rosvooruzhenie, Russia's eight exporting companies sold about $3 billion-worth of arms in 1995, with Rosvooruzhenie accounting for 90% of this total. See interview with Rosvooruzehnie's First Deputy Director-General Oleg Sidorenko, *Finansovaya Izvestiya*, 29 October 1996.
[34] *The Military Balance 1996/97*, p. 275.
[35] Sherman Garnett, 'Russia's

Illusory Ambitions', *Foreign Affairs*, vol. 76, no. 2, March/April 1997, p. 65.
[36] Malcolm, Pravda, Allison and Light, *Internal Factors in Russian Foreign Policy*, pp. 183–84.
[37] Interview with First Deputy Minister for the Fuel and Power Industry Anatoly Shatanov, *Argumenty i Fakty*, no. 47, 1996.
[38] Garnett, 'Russia's Illusory Ambitions', pp. 62–76.
[39] Kozyrev, *Preobrazhenie*, pp. 240–41. Kozyrev emphasised that Siberia and the Far East will provide Russia's economic channel to the Asia-Pacific; that Moscow's Far Eastern policy should focus on internal economic development; and that diplomacy should be used to create the most favourable political conditions for such development.

Chapter 2

[1] See Table 8, p. 32.
[2] See, for example, Yang Chengxu, Director of the Institute for International Studies, Beijing, in 'Chinese Scholars Review 1996', *Beijing Review*, vol. 40, no. 4, 27 January–2 February 1997, p. 7.
[3] The English text of the Joint Statement quoted in this section is based on the version published in *Beijing Review*, vol. 39, 13–19 May 1996, pp. 6–8.
[4] Natalia Pulia and Alexander Reutov, 'An Agreement Conceived in the Soviet Period was Signed with China Yesterday', *Nezavisimaya Gazeta*, 25 April 1997; Robin Lodge, 'Ex-Soviet States and China Sign Deal on Frontier Troop Cuts', *The Times*, 25 April 1997.
[5] Interview with Primakov, 'Yevgeni Primakov Talks about

Russia's Foreign Policy', *Rossiiskaya Gazeta*, 10 January 1997.
[6] *The Military Balance 1996/97*, pp. 171 and 181.
[7] 'Russia and China Attempt to Balance US Power', *International Herald Tribune*, 28–29 December 1996.
[8] Figures calculated from *Direction of Trade Statistics Yearbook* (Washington DC: International Monetary Fund, 1996).
[9] For more details, see Nathalie de Spiegeleire, *Chinese Immigration to Siberia: The Impact on Regional Stability* (Ebenhausen: Stiftung Wissenschaft und Politik, 1995).
[10] *People's Daily*, 28 December 1996.
[11] *Beijing Review*, vol. 40, 12–18 May 1997, pp. 78.
[12] *Asahi Shimbun*, 18 May 1997, p. 2.
[13] *International Herald Tribune*, 28–29 December 1996.

Chapter 3

[1] For Japanese views of Russia, see Hiroshi Kimura, 'Japanese Perceptions of Russia', in James E. Goodby, Vladimir I. Ivanov and Nobuo Shimotomai (eds), *'Northern Territories' and Beyond* (Westport, CT: Praeger, 1995), pp. 55–62; Shigeki Hakamada, 'Five Issues in the Improvement of Russo-Japanese Relations', *Gaiko Forum*, no. 98, October 1996, pp. 29–39.
[2] For Russian views of Japan, see Semiyon I. Verbitskii, 'Russian Perceptions of Japan', in Goodby, Ivanov and Shimotomai, *'Northern Territories' and Beyond*, pp. 63–69.
[3] Komachi, 'Concept-Building in Russian Diplomacy', p. 4.
[4] *Ibid.*, p. 2.
[5] *Komsomolskaya Pravda*, 27 May 1992.
[6] Kozyrev, *Preobrazhenie*, p. 244.

[7] For a Japanese policy-maker's view of Mikhail Gorbachev's visit to Japan, see Kazuhiko Togo, *Nichi-Ro Shinjidai-eno Jyosou* (Tokyo: Simul Press, 1993).
[8] For the term 'principle of expanded equilibrium', see *ibid.*, pp. 24–25 and 169–70.
[9] Ministry of Foreign Affairs of Japan, Secretariat of the Cooperation Committee, 'Japan's Assistance to the New Independent States, Fact Sheet', Tokyo, Ministry of Foreign Affairs, April 1996, p. 16.
[10] *Asahi Shimbun*, 20 April 1996, p. 1.
[11] Interview with Primakov, 'Yevgeni Primakov Talks About Russia's Foreign Policy'.
[12] *Asahi Shimbun*, 16 November 1996, p. 2.
[13] *RIA Novosti*, 6 March 1997.
[14] The four disputed islands are known as the 'South Kuril Islands' by Russia and the 'Northern Territories' by Japan.
[15] *Nikkei Shimbun*, 21 March 1996, p. 2.
[16] All figures are based on trade statistics published annually by Japan's Ministry of Finance.
[17] *Ibid.*, and see Table 2, p. 22.
[18] Based on trade statistics published annually by Japan's Ministry of Finance.
[19] 'Round Table, The Economy of Far Eastern Russia: High Expectations of Japan', *Gaiko Forum*, no. 98, October 1996, p. 56.
[20] *Nikkei Shimbun*, 21 March 1996, p. 1.
[21] *Defense of Japan*, pp. 163–64.
[22] *Asahi Shimbun*, 18 May 1997, p. 2.

Chapter 4

[1] Segal, *The Soviet Union and the Pacific*, p. 99.
[2] Gorbachev, *Gorbachev Kaisouroku*,

p. 536. This discussion appears in the Japanese-language version, but not in the English-language version.

[3] 'Agreed Framework Between the Democratic People's Republic of Korea and the United States of America', signed in Geneva, 21 October 1994.

[4] Interview with Andrei Kozyrev, *Izvestiya*, 18 June 1994.

[5] *Russia Today*, 2 December 1996.

[6] Sergei Mushkaterov, 'Moscow Stops Selling Offensive Weapons to DPRK', *Izvestiya*, 19 March 1992, in *The Current Digest of the Post-Soviet Press*, vol. 44, no. 11, 1992, p. 16.

[7] Vasily Koronenko, 'In Seoul, Yeltsin Proposes 23 Projects for Economic Cooperation with South Korea', *Izvestiya*, 19 November 1992, in *The Current Digest of the Post-Soviet Press*, vol. 44, no. 46, 1992, pp. 15–16.

[8] RFE/RFL, *Daily Report*, 3 June 1994.

[9] 'The Bazaar Syndrome, or How We Do Business With South Korea', *Rossiiskie Vesti*, 7 February 1995, in *The Current Digest of the Post-Soviet Press*, vol. 47, no. 6, 1995, pp. 29–30.

[10] *Izvestiya*, 19 November and 20 December 1992.

[11] *Izvestiya*, 1 December 1993.

[12] *Yomiuri Shimbun*, 7 September 1994, p. 5.

[13] *Finansovye Ivestiya*, 13 July 1995.

[14] 'US Warns Seoul on Russian Missiles', *International Herald Tribune*, 7 April 1997, p. 4.

[15] *Mainichi Shimbun*, 23 May 1995, p. 6.

[16] *Diplomaticheskaya Vesnik*, no. 10, 1995, p. 15.

[17] Georgy Stepanov, 'Russia Does Not Want to Make a One-Sided Choice in Seoul's Favour', *Izvestiya*, 31 July 1992.

[18] Sergei Agafanov and Igor Golembiovsky, 'Without Illusions But With Hope for the Future', *Izvestiya*, 12 November 1992, in *The Current Digest of the Post-Soviet Press*, vol. 44, no. 46, 1992, pp. 13–15.

[19] Aleksandr Zhebin and Vadim Tkachenko, 'Kunadze Flies to Pyongyang via Beijing', *Nezavisimaya Gazeta*, 17 February 1993, in *The Current Digest of the Post-Soviet Press*, vol. 45, no. 8, 1993, pp. 13–14.

[20] Vladislav Chernov, 'Russia's National Interests and Threats to its Security', *Nezavisimaya Gazeta*, 29 April 1993, in *The Current Digest of the Post-Soviet Press*, vol. 45, no. 17, 1993, pp. 13–15.

Conclusion

[1] Yukio Satoh, *Policy Coordination for Asia-Pacific Security and Stability*, Working Paper 305 (Canberra: Strategic and Defence Studies Center, Australian National University, 1996), pp. 12–15.

[2] During his February 1997 visit to London, Russian Foreign Minister Yevgeni Primakov addressed the issue of NATO enlargement. He publicly warned that Russia was deliberately shifting its attention away from the West towards other areas including China, India, Japan, Latin America and the Middle East. See 'Kremlin Begins to Bargain Over NATO Expansion', *The Times*, 1 March 1997.

[3] Jack F. Matrock, Jr, 'Dealing with a Russia in Turmoil', *Foreign Affairs*, vol. 75, no. 3, May/June 1996, p. 51.

For Product Safety Concerns and Information please contact our EU
representative GPSR@taylorandfrancis.com
Taylor & Francis Verlag GmbH, Kaufingerstraße 24, 80331 München, Germany

www.ingramcontent.com/pod-product-compliance
Ingram Content Group UK Ltd.
Pitfield, Milton Keynes, MK11 3LW, UK
UKHW021437080625
459435UK00011B/282